word of GOD, word of LIFE

word of GOD, word of LIFE

Understanding the Three-Year Lectionaries

GAIL RAMSHAW

AUGSBURG FORTRESS

WORD OF GOD, WORD OF LIFE
Understanding the Three-Year Lectionaries

Cover design: Laurie Ingram
Cover image: © John Coburn / Copyright Agency. Licensed by Artists
Rights Society (ARS), New York, 2019.
Interior images: Tanja Butler, Julie Lonneman, Nicholas Markell,
Lucinda Naylor, and Gertrud Mueller Nelson from sundaysandseasons.com
© Augsburg Fortress.
Interior design and typesetting: Tory Herman
Editor: Laurie J. Hanson

Manufactured in the U.S.A.

pISBN 978-1-5064-4915-9
eISBN 978-1-5064-4916-6

26 25 24 23 22 21 20 19   1 2 3 4 5 6 7 8 9 10

Contents

Introduction

IDENTIFYING THE
THREE-YEAR LECTIONARIES

How sweet are your words to my taste,
sweeter than honey to my mouth! . . .
Your word is a lamp to my feet
and a light to my path. . . .
You are my hiding place and my shield;
I hope in your word.

Psalm 119:103, 105, 114

Around the world, especially on Sundays, Christians assemble to honor God, to listen to readings from their sacred scriptures, and to share a holy meal of bread and wine. When a biblical reading is completed at these gatherings, it has become common for the reader to call out, "The word of the Lord," to which the worshipers respond, "Thanks be to God." More than sixteen centuries ago, Augustine described these very scriptures in this way: "I therefore decided to give attention to the holy scriptures and to find out what they were like. And this is what met me: a text lowly to the beginner but, on further reading, of mountainous difficulty and enveloped in mysteries."[1] Yet at weekly worship, despite at least some selections being "of mountainous difficulty and enveloped in mysteries," the baptized community receives these passages, acclaims them as the "word of God," and praises God for the gift of this word.

What do Christians mean by the phrases "the word of the Lord" and "the word of God"? Especially over the last two hundred years, some Christians have suggested that "word of God" means that God dictated the words of the Bible: the scriptural authors were channeling the voice of God; thus the Bible—at least in its original languages of Hebrew and Greek—is inerrant. However, throughout Christian history, the meaning of these phrases has been more complex. It is as if the designation "the word of God" is a door that opens to the faithful a crowded dining room filled with conversations about divine mystery. Christians believe that never throughout human history was God silent. Rather, God's continuous activity in the universe and among believers has been described as speech: God is heard in words of mercy and challenge, not only within the human heart, but primarily through the texts of the Bible.

. . . .

During the twentieth century, a phenomenal consensus across denominational boundaries brought about the widespread use of a single lectionary family, designated in this volume as "the three-year lectionaries."

. . . .

In Genesis 1, God speaks words and so creates the world, and repeatedly in the scriptures God speaks to persons by name and calls them into ministry. The prologue of the fourth gospel calls Jesus the very Word of God, and Christians believe that this Word continues to talk to and with the faithful through the power of the Holy Spirit. Referring to the Bible as "the word of God" is thus a shorthand way to give the highest honor to these many ancient writings. Although biblical writings were crafted over a millennium by a motley crew of forebears in the faith, with all the authors writing for their own time and place, the church judges them as continuously invaluable. The will and the ways of God are still heard today by the faithful in, with, and under the texts of these scriptures. Revered as "the word of God," the scriptural passages affirm that the presence of God in the assembly is assured.

For which biblical readings does the assembly offer thanks to God? How were the readings for worship chosen? In order to determine which religious material was suitable and efficacious for public reading, first Jews and then Christians chose the individual books that together became the Bible. Thus the function of the Bible from its inception was "lectionary"; that is, the writings were chosen as appropriate for public proclamation during communal worship. (The noun *lectionary* is also used to designate a ritual book in which the biblical readings for worship are bound sequentially, to assist the reader in public worship. However, in this volume, *lectionary* carries the meaning of the list of biblical selections intended for public worship that is utilized by one or more ecclesial communities.)

In some ecclesial communities, the preacher is expected personally to choose an appropriate "word of God" for each worship event. Sermons extant from the early centuries of the church, however, suggest that at least as early as the fourth century for the primary festivals, the choice of appropriate biblical readings was shared from one Christian community to another. Fuller lectionaries began to appear in the fifth century, although without the kind of commentary that we would appreciate as to why certain passages were chosen and others omitted. Scholars agree that the Christian practice of selecting various passages from throughout the scriptures, rather than of reading sequentially through each book, meant that for public worship the codex—what we call a book—was more practical than the scroll, and this preference led subsequently to the dominance of the book format for all purposes throughout society. Over later centuries, it was often the case that one group of Christians could be distinguished from another by its lectionary, its leaders having made decisions as to which biblical readings were more essential than others for the people's belief and practice.

During the twentieth century, a phenomenal consensus across denominational boundaries brought about the widespread use of a single lectionary family, designated in this volume as "the three-year lectionaries." On this single lectionary tree are several major branches. The *Ordo Lectionum Missae*, the parent of this three-year system, was the work of a Roman Catholic committee authorized for its momentous creative task by the Second Vatican Council. First promulgated in 1969, this Lectionary for

Mass (LM) is canonically required for use by Roman Catholics in the United States in a 1998 version and in Canada in a 1992 version; other regional variations exist.[2]

The brilliance of this lectionary inspired some Protestants to shape their own adaptations of it. Given denominationally differing hermeneutics, there arose an increasing number of variants of the LM. This led in 1983 to a version upon which several Protestant churches collaborated, and this ongoing cooperation culminated finally in the 1992 Revised Common Lectionary (RCL).[3] This ecumenical offering was not intended as an inviolate rule for worship, but rather as a proposal to the many Protestant churches: the RCL provided a common approach to the weekly proclamation of the Bible, while leaving room for decisions related to denominational calendars and concerns. Increasingly in use around the world,[4] the RCL in some churches is canonically required, in others is standard practice, and in still others is advice meant to inform local decisions for preaching.[5]

Both the LM and the RCL regularize the practice of reading not only from first-century Christian writings, but also from the sacred texts of Judaism. In reaction against centuries of anti-Semitism in church and society, Christians have become aware of the dangers inherent in their use of the Hebrew scriptures, and some suggest that the very term *Old Testament* be replaced.[6] Yet Christians mean to affirm that the Hebrew scriptures are also their parental texts, the essential initial source of their testimony to Christ, the "old" without which the "new" would be incomprehensible.[7] Thus, as the conversation about terminology continues among Christians, this volume will generally refer to the Christian use of the Hebrew scriptures as their Old Testament.

Because the Protestants who designed the RCL brought to their collaborative task their own historically grounded hermeneutical differences, especially when considering how the Old Testament ought to be proclaimed in Sunday worship, the RCL includes two tracks for the non-festival half of the year, from Trinity Sunday through the last Sunday of the liturgical year. One track is called "complementary" (hereafter in this volume "RCL*") and always in some way ties the Old Testament reading to the gospel selection.[8] The other track is called "semicontinuous" (hereafter in this volume

"RCL+") and for half of the year reads more or less sequentially, following a proposed historical order of events, through parts of the Old Testament.[9] Other slightly emended forms of the RCL have been developed by several Protestant denominations for use by their own members.

In all the variants of this lectionary family, readings are appointed for the historic seasons of Advent, Christmas, Lent, and Easter; for three years of Sundays; and for the non-Sunday festivals of Christmas Eve, Christmas Day, Epiphany, Ash Wednesday, the Triduum (Holy Thursday, Good Friday, and the Easter Vigil), Ascension, and All Saints. The LM also includes readings for many explicitly Roman Catholic days and occasions, while the RCL includes Presentation, Annunciation, Visitation, Holy Cross, and Thanksgiving. Some churches have added their own favored Sundays and festivals to their practice. For example, some Lutherans keep Reformation Sunday with its own set of biblical readings.

Although the majority of readings are held in common, some differences between the LM and RCL are apparent. Often the RCL appoints a longer reading than does the LM. The various church bodies also use their own distinctive labels for Sundays and feasts, so that what for some churches is the "Nativity of the Lord" or the "Nativity of Our Lord Jesus Christ," is for others the "Birth of the Lord, Christmas Day." Consecutive Sundays during non-festival times of the year are numbered differently, so that the ninth Sunday in ordinary time in the LM is Proper 4 in the RCL. These variations make the ecumenical use of liturgical resources something of a challenge. In addition, some differences in readings correspond to the churches' characteristic emphases. For example, on one Sunday, illustrative of Roman Catholic reverence for Peter, the LM readings include Acts 5:15, which speaks of those who were sick hoping that Peter's shadow would fall on them. On the same Sunday, illustrative of Protestant emphasis on preaching, the RCL reading quotes instead the preaching of Peter and the apostles in Acts 5:29-32.

Some studies discussing this lectionary family have stressed the historic hermeneutical differences between Roman Catholics and those Protestants who are now committed to the use of a common lectionary system.[10]

Although on occasion this volume will comment on the differences within this lectionary family, the intention here is not to dwell on these differences, but rather to emphasize the commonality of proclamation of this lectionary family throughout the world. As the First Ecumenical Imperative recently proposed by Roman Catholics and Lutherans states, churches are to "always begin from the perspective of unity and not from the point of view of division in order to strengthen what is held in common even though the differences are more easily seen and experienced."[11] There is currently around the world a tendency to promote one's own distinctive identity, rather than any shared humanity. To counter this narrow practice, one way that Christians can celebrate the unity God promises to the church throughout the world is a willing agreement to read the Bible in similar ways at Sunday worship and to rejoice in that commonality.

Several denominations and religious publishing houses provide impressive commentaries on this lectionary system, offering weekly exegetical assistance and suggestions for sermon preparation, as well as for liturgical complements in music, art, and action.[12] Much of this material meets specifically denominational interests and preferences, and the vast amount and high quality of these liturgical resources are in themselves praiseworthy contributions to the worship life of twenty-first-century churches. Given all these notable materials, this volume need not proceed week by week through the three years with homily helps and liturgical suggestions.

Rather, this volume attends to the underlying principles upon which this family of lectionaries is constructed. Many persons who utilize these lectionaries remain unaware of such principles, and thus they cannot capitalize on them to maximize the meaning of the appointed selections. Of such minimal understanding of the logic behind this lectionary system, the lectionary scholar Fritz West wrote, "Such uses are like playing checkers with a chess set."[13] However, it is the hope of this volume that increased attention to the lectionaries' foundational principles will assist all interested Christians in the weekly task of biblical interpretation for the life of the church: both preachers and hearers will understand why the chess pieces are placed where they are, what is their interrelationship with each other, and which are designed to exert dominance over others.

Each of the ten chapters in this book addresses one foundational principle. Chapter 1 addresses the first and primary hermeneutical principle of this lectionary family: that for Christians, every Sunday is resurrection day. This emphasis on Christ's resurrection is manifest especially during the fifty days of Easter. Chapter 2 focuses on the gospel reading for the day and illustrates principle 2 especially in the season of Christmas. Chapter 3 addresses the Old Testament reading, chapter 4 the assembly's singing of the psalms, and chapter 5 the second reading's use of New Testament writings. The principles discussed in chapters 6 and 7 apply to the seasons of Advent and Lent. Chapter 8 deals with Holy Week, the Triduum, and Easter Day. Chapter 9 demonstrates how the Trinity permeates the entire lectionary, and chapter 10 attends to the worldwide Christian unity that this lectionary provides. The conclusion addresses some of the criticisms raised against the three-year lectionaries, including the perceived anti-Semitism of the Holy Week readings in particular.

. . . .

One way that Christians can celebrate the unity God promises to the church throughout the world is a willing agreement to read the Bible in similar ways at Sunday worship and to rejoice in that commonality.

. . . .

Each chapter opens with a biblical citation, indicating that the ten principles derive from the Bible itself, and a summary statement of the foundational principle at hand. From there each chapter is divided into three parts. The first part presents a theological and liturgical exposition of the principle, based on both the church year and the biblical books from which the readings come. The second part looks at the principle in wider context, as described in the next paragraph. The third part analyzes several samples from the lectionaries that illustrate the principle. For example, according to principle 1, the three-year lectionaries understand every Sunday to proclaim the death and resurrection of Christ; this principle helps to determine each week's readings over the three years. One obvious example of this principle is seen on the second Sunday of Easter; a more obscure example is the Sunday on which the severe parable of the king's wedding banquet in Matthew 22:1-14 is proclaimed.

The second half of the title of this volume is "Word of Life." As an optional response to the Sunday biblical readings, the primary worship resource used by many North American Lutherans offers the phrase "Word of God, word of life," to which the assembly responds, "Thanks be to God."[14] The scripture readings are the "word of life" for us in two ways. Not only do these biblical texts apply to all of life, serving both as the foundation of our days and the windows for our vision, but these words also offer the life of God to the whole of our existence. In this study of the three-year lectionaries, all ten principles are shown not only to strengthen Christian faith but also to connect with the daily ordinary worldview of many twenty-first-century people. The second part of each chapter considers this value hidden within the lectionaries' principles. For example, Sunday worship that attends to Christ's resurrection is seen as an example of human ritual, and enacting such ritual is shown to have substantive value for the individual and the community. It is hoped that these nonreligious psychological and social parallels to the church's situation might prove interesting also to persons who are not worshiping Christians.

Other lectionary systems are utilized around the world. Quite different from the lectionaries of churches in the West, the one-year lectionary maintained by the Eastern Orthodox churches is treasured because it is ancient, rather than because it is continuously updated.[15] During the twentieth century several Protestant churches expanded the medieval one-year Western lectionary into a two- or three-year system, in which subsequent years mimic the logic of the one-year pattern.[16] These lectionaries, even if they are three years long, are not part of the single lectionary family that is addressed in this volume. Yet other lectionaries—some rather idiosyncratic, some with narrow purpose—are currently in use. Perhaps this volume will help to inspire their users to adopt or adapt instead this three-year lectionary system, and thus to participate with millions of other Christians in a worldwide unity in proclaiming the word of the Lord.

The cover art by John Coburn titled "Transfiguration, 1979" can be seen as a graphic depiction of the exuberant vitality of the proclamation of the word: the readings from the New Testament, especially the four gospels, and from the Old Testament circle around Christ, who is always the center; together the readings hover over what recalls both the font and the chalice; and all around springs forth life—trees and leaves and seeds of color—in places both nearby and distant.

This book has been written by a laywoman, who never preaches in the assembly, for all worshipers, both clergy and laity. The author knew from early childhood that the lectionary listing, which was provided in the front pages of the hymnal held in everyone's hands, was God's gift not merely for preachers, but for all the baptized. As a septuagenarian, this author believes that the more preparation we all can bring to Sunday morning, the more intentional might be our response, "Thanks be to God."

NOTES

1   Augustine, *Confessions*, III v. 9, trans. Henry Chadwick (Oxford, UK: Oxford University Press, 1991), 40.

2   See *Lectionary for Mass,* study ed., vol. 1: *Sundays, Solemnities, Feasts of the Lord and the Saints* (Collegeville, MN: Liturgical Press, 2000). For a comparison between the USA and Canadian versions, see 1273-83. For a detailed explanation of the committee's work, see Normand Bonneau, *The Sunday Lectionary: Ritual Word, Paschal Shape* (Collegeville, MN: Liturgical Press, 1998), 21-55.

3   See Consultation on Common Texts, *The Revised Common Lectionary,* 20th-anniversary annotated ed. (Minneapolis: Fortress, 2012). For a detailed explanation of the formation of the Revised Common Lectionary, see Horace T. Allen Jr. and Joseph P. Russell, *On Common Ground: The Story of the Revised Common Lectionary* (Norwich, UK: Canterbury, 1998), 3-12.

4   For a reasonably accurate listing of the churches that support the Revised Common Lectionary, see "The Consultation on Common Texts," www.commontexts.org.

5   See Thomas O'Loughlin, *Making the Most of the Lectionary: A User's Guide* (London: SPCK, 2012), for a persuasive defense of the lectionary, given critical reactions to it.

6   See Gail Ramshaw, "The First Testament in Christian Lectionaries," *Worship* 64 (1990): 494-510, for a sustained discussion of this question.

7   See Gordon W. Lathrop, *Saving Images: The Presence of the Bible in Christian Liturgy* (Minneapolis: Fortress, 2017), 50-51.

8   For a discussion of this method, see Gail Ramshaw, *A Three-Year Banquet: The Lectionary for the Assembly* (Minneapolis: Augsburg Fortress, 2004), 47-54.

9   For a discussion of this method, see Peter C. Bower, ed., *Handbook for the Revised Common Lectionary* (Louisville: Westminster John Knox, 1996), 8-13.

10 See Fritz West, *Scripture and Memory: The Ecumenical Hermeneutic of the Three-Year Lectionaries* (Collegeville, MN: Liturgical Press, 1997) and Victoria Raymer, *The Bible in Worship: Proclamation, Encounters and Response* (London: SCM, 2018), especially "The Synoptic Lectionaries: Characteristics," 162-77.

11 Lutheran-Roman Catholic Commission on Unity. *From Conflict to Communion: Lutheran-Catholic Common Commemoration of the Reformation in 2017* (Leipzig: Evangelische Verlagsanstalt, 2013), par. 239, #87.

12 See the bibliography for a list of the most impressive of many print and online lectionary guides now available.

13 West, *Scripture and Memory*, 183.

14 *Evangelical Lutheran Worship* (Minneapolis: Augsburg Fortress, 2006), 102, 124.

15 See Georges Barrois, *Scripture Readings in Orthodox Worship* (Crestwood, NY: St. Vladimir's Seminary Press, 1977).

16 See, for example, Nils-Henrik Nilsson, "The Principles behind the New Sunday Lectionary for the Church of Sweden," *Studia Liturgica* 34 (Sept. 2004): 240-50.

Principle 1

ABOUT SUNDAY AND CHRIST'S RESURRECTION

When it was evening on that day, the first day of the week, and the doors of the house where the disciples had met were locked for fear of the Jews, Jesus came and stood among them and said, "Peace be with you." . . . A week later his disciples were again in the house, and Thomas was with them. Although the doors were shut, Jesus came and stood among them and said, "Peace be with you."

John 20:19, 26

. . . .

1 The fundamental Christian ritual is held on Sunday, because Sunday is the day of Christ's resurrection. In the three-year lectionaries, the resurrection undergirds every Sunday, as well as the fifty days of the Easter season.

Principle 1 in the lectionary

The Bible makes minimum reference to a weekly Christian ritual.[1] Paul wrote to the Christians in Corinth that "on the first day of every week," perhaps at some such meeting, believers were to collect money for the needs of the saints (1 Cor. 16:1-2). The book of Acts describes an event "on the first day of the week, when we met to break bread" (Acts 20:7). The visions of the Johannine seer of Revelation are said to have occurred "on the Lord's day" (Rev. 1:10), and the Johannine author of the Gospel of John narrated meetings a week apart at which the risen Christ appeared (John 20:19, 26-27). So although there is much we do not know about precisely when, how, and why the Christian weekly meeting came about, scholars concur that by the end of the first century, Christians were assembling on Sunday to hear the word of God and to share a holy meal.[2] By the fourth century, Christians had come to title their day of meeting "Sunday" and to connect the light of Christ with the sun.[3]

However, the earliest title that Christians gave to the day of meeting seems to have been "the Lord's Day," meaning the day on which the Lord Jesus rose from the dead.[4] This early pattern of acclaiming Jesus as "Lord" articulates the primary credo of the baptized: that the honorific normally granted to God is now to be used also for the risen Christ. As one historian wrote, "Although the mood and many rituals of the Lord's Day were borrowed from Judaism and elsewhere, they were meant to have specific Christian purpose: namely, reinforcing Jesus' resurrection through fellowship with him (believed to be present) and with other believers."[5] Quite simply, the determinative for Christian faith and practice was not knowledge about Jesus' life and ministry or maintenance of a certain ethical lifestyle, but rather the communal belief, exercised through a weekly ritual meeting, that Christ's death and resurrection constitute the crux of human history and the salvation of individual life.[6] Worship at the outset of each week symbolized the ordering of one's entire life under the cross.

Another early title given to the day of meeting was "the first day," a way to recall God's creation of the world and thus to suggest that in the resurrection of Christ, the world had been created anew, a new world begun. Yet another designation was "the eighth day," a metaphor borrowed from Jewish apocalyptic writings that conveyed the hope that when this world would come to its violent end, God would establish a new time beyond current reckoning. For Christians, baptism was entry into this new time, which replaced the evils and sorrows of the old world by the power of God's Spirit. Thus the several titles given to the weekly ritual of meeting on each Sunday carried a trinitarian resonance: on "the first day," God recreated the world; on "the Lord's day," Christ rose from death; and on "the eighth day," the Spirit of God brought about the baptism of a new people for a new age.[7]

. . . .

Worship at the outset of each week symbolized the ordering of one's entire life under the cross.

. . . .

Throughout the centuries, Christians have read from the immensely long Bible with various objectives. They may have been in search of personal comfort, private spirituality, heartfelt poetry, engaging narrative, moral inspiration, social critique, or lyrics for song. In our time they may be looking for examples of ancient mythology, indications of ancient Near Eastern history, or the purported records of, say, the role of women in the past. They may be comparing and contrasting the Bible with other sacred texts. They may be hunting for correctives to their denominational emphases, for passages overlooked in their current practice, or for those embarrassing parts of the Bible that they never heard about in Sunday school. But regardless of the many reasons Christians read the Bible, our interest in this volume is lectionary—what Justin Martyr referred to in about the year 150, that when believers assembled on "the day that is named after the sun . . . the records of the apostles or the writings of the prophets are read for as long as there is time."[8]

The primary reason that the Christian writings were collected into what became our Bible was to provide a library of texts available for public reading at weekly worship.[9] For example, we read aloud the story of creation from Genesis 1, rather than the far more complex narrative from the Book of Jubilees. For proclamation on Sunday, our canon of scripture includes the four gospels, not all those noncanonical writings now readily available online. This selection process took some time: disputes arose for several hundred years about which books ought to receive status as scriptural canon. The earliest extant list of what is precisely our New Testament is credited to Athanasius in 367.

From the earliest days of the church, leaders selected passages from those preferred books as the focus of their preaching. One might think about these selections as the crucial Bible, those passages read aloud in worship because they were judged essential for the faith and nurture of believers. For example, at worship Christians have read aloud the tale in Genesis 3 of "the fall" of the first humans in the garden, but have not proclaimed the odd passage in Genesis 6 about sexual intercourse between the "sons of God" and human females.

. . . .

Those who designed the lectionary intended that all readings in some way point to the death and resurrection of Christ.

. . . .

This selection process constituting a Christian lectionary is not to deny the value of other parts of the Bible, nor the good that results from other uses of the scriptures. But it does suggest that the desire of some of the later reformers, that the entire Bible be read through week by week, was unrealistic as to how sacred writings might best serve the entire worshiping community. For example, the regulations in Leviticus 13–14 about how to deal with leprosy, whether it infects humans or produces "greenish or reddish spots" (14:37) on the walls of a house, have been rightly judged as immaterial to the contemporary faith of Christians and thus are not appointed in lectionaries. Yet to appreciate the narratives of Jesus' association with persons afflicted with leprosy, some biblical understanding of the disease is helpful. Any lectionary system, whether personally compiled by a preacher or adopted for use by a church body, represents a judgment about which parts of the massive library of biblical books are most essential for the faithful to receive on the primary day of the religious assembly.

In constructing a lectionary, one might aim toward various goals. Perhaps the primary goal is evangelistic outreach.[10] A lectionary might focus on teaching a biblical time line of history.[11] A lectionary might focus on personal spiritual growth. A lectionary might attend largely to contemporary moral concerns. In any case, a lectionary committee must decide whether there is value in reading from as many biblical books as possible. It is interesting to examine the lectionary as used by contemporary Amish Christians in Lancaster County, Pennsylvania.[12] Gathering for worship as they do only every other week, their one-year lectionary selects from only ten New Testament books. Half of the readings come from Matthew, a gospel that is keen on obedience, and from Luke, a gospel that stresses forgiveness. It matters—what is in one's lectionary.

In contrast to other imagined or genuine lectionary schemes, the fundamental organizing principle for the three-year lectionary we are considering is the pattern of the early church: We meet on Sunday to affirm the resurrection of Christ for the life of the world. Christians assemble weekly around word and sacrament as the foundation of their identity and the impetus for ethical living. Each week of our lives is guided by the Spirit of the risen Christ, the days of each week renewed by means of the ritual of praise and petition. Thus, those who designed the lectionary intended that all readings in some way point to the death and resurrection of Christ. One presider's prayer that is appointed for every regular Sunday of the year says it this way: that Jesus Christ "on this day overcame death and the grave."[13] That is, every Sunday is the day of the resurrection, and we read from the Bible accordingly at our weekly meeting.

Naturally, there is ecumenical diversity in how various users of this lectionary family focus on Christ. In one guide to the RCL with authors from both the Anglican and the Reformed traditions, the Anglican elucidating his use of the RCL described a "typically Anglican point of view: Our salvation is rooted in the Incarnation. That means that salvation comes in and through our physical, particular, and historical living."[14] Meanwhile, the coauthor wrote, "The biblical texts tell the story of the presence and work of God in and through history, in and through specific communities of faith. . . . My Reformed orientation and understanding of the centrality of the biblical story lead me to start with the specifics of the biblical text."[15] Thus, the advocates of this lectionary employ various lenses through which they proclaim the word of God, the word of life. But whichever the preferred hermeneutic, the lectionaries intend to bring into the present the transformative power of Christ. For example, the gospel reading on the Sunday of Mark 2:1-12 proclaims Christ as the healer, not only then, but now. During his ministry Jesus healed a man of paralysis, and now he heals us; he granted forgiveness during his ministry, and now at this liturgy he forgives us.

For annual festivals, both those on Sunday and those on certain dates of the year, the lectionary utilizes the traditional pattern called *lectio selecta*. Holy Week and Easter constitute the high point of the liturgical year. This conviction echoes the Western pattern in the Middle Ages when the sign of faithful church membership was attendance at Easter worship following obligatory penance during Lent. Although in some times and places Good Friday has been observed in deepest mourning, in this lectionary family—even on the day of Jesus' death—Christians know that he is raised, and thus, the gospel reading for Good Friday is the passion according to John, in which the divine Christ is victorious, reigning from the cross. Even the narratives proclaimed at Epiphany point to his coming death and resurrection: King Herod was unsuccessful in killing the infant Jesus, but Pilate looms always before us, in our collective memory and in our baptismal creed.[16]

In all three years, usually designated as year A, year B, and year C, the passages chosen for non-festival Sundays travel more or less semicontinuously through the gospels in a pattern historically called *lectio continua*. Given the nature of the selections, each Sunday can stand independently from its neighbors, each Sunday being a little Easter—a lectionary pattern useful in our time when attendance at worship for many church members is more monthly than weekly. The goal that even standard Sundays proclaim the salvation of Christ through the Spirit is achieved through several means.

First, the primary reading is understood to be the one taken from one of the four gospels (see chapter 2). In some church traditions, the assembly stands to hear this reading in a symbolic posture of respect. Believers assemble in the first place to be strengthened by the presence of Christ in the assembly, and only secondarily for the myriad other interests that draw Christians to worship.

Second, any passage from the four gospels is not to be viewed in isolation from the book from which it comes. In the late nineteenth century Martin Kähler proposed that the gospels are long prefaces added to the accounts of the passion, death, and resurrection of Christ.[17] Every selection from the gospels in some way leads the church to Holy Week and Easter. For example, the passages in Matthew 13 and Mark 4 about the mustard seed could be used to illustrate what English teachers used to call "the wide truths of life," that little beginnings may grow to great ends. But in the New Testament, a reference to the surprising valuation of what might be overlooked inevitably points to Christ, and so in the lectionary the mustard bush can be seen as a metaphor for the cross. The cross and empty tomb are there, on a regular Sunday. The Christian proclamation is both simple—the same every Sunday—and evermore immeasurable—always more layered, cumulative, profound, week after week, year after year.

Yet a third feature of the three-year lectionaries assists each set of readings in proclaiming the death and resurrection of Christ. The Roman Catholics who designed the LM and a growing number of the Protestants who advocate for the RCL agree on this: that the Christian assembly on every Sunday includes the sacrament of holy communion. One goal of the biblical readings is to lead toward and complement the upcoming communion. If the biblical readings have been chosen toward some other purpose, or if the preaching has veered away from proclaiming salvation in the triune God, then the ritual of eucharist may have little or no connection with the readings, and the primary goal of assembling for word and sacrament has been obscured.

That the lectionary desires the faithful participation of all the baptized every Sunday corresponds with our knowledge about rituals—that religions rely on repeated, symbolic, communal activity to articulate their beliefs and to strengthen the bonds both between the divine and the human and among the community members. Despite the benefits of individual meditation on the Bible, we do not become Christians by ourselves, and the advocates of the lectionary agree that thanks to the weekly ritual, with the regular repetition of the faith and with its layered symbolic expressions of that faith, the religious community comes more and more to be what it is, the body of the risen Christ for the life of the world.

That the three-year lectionaries appoint Easter as lasting fifty days epitomizes the Christian focus on the resurrection. Easter Day is only the beginning of the story. On the second Sunday of Easter, the risen Christ appears to a wider group of disciples. On the third Sunday, more resurrection appearances are narrated. John 10 is divided up over the three years of the fourth Sunday to apply the imagery of the good shepherd to the risen Christ. On the fifth and sixth Sundays, passages from John 14–15 testify to the ongoing power of the Spirit of the risen Christ in the baptized community. On the seventh Sunday, John 17, a prayer ascribed to Jesus on the night before his crucifixion, speaks to the whole church in light of the resurrection. Thus although all four gospels proclaim the resurrection, during the Easter season the lectionaries look especially to the Gospel according to John to unfold the mystery of that event.

Two related matters: What about a weekly ritual on a day other than Sunday? Roman Catholics have provided for those whose work schedules conflict with Sunday participation by sanctioning weekly worship also on Saturday evening. In this way, following ancient precedent, Saturday sundown is viewed as the onset of Sunday. Thus in Roman Catholic churches, the Sunday readings appointed in the LM are used also for the Saturday evening "vigil" masses. However, during the twentieth century, many Protestant churches came to schedule a midweek service as an option to Sunday worship. Characteristically, these services are scheduled on Wednesday, and they may use the Sunday lectionary of either of the adjacent Sundays. For Christians, however, it would be more profound to schedule any such midweek worship on Thursday. Wednesday brings with it no particular resonance of Christ. However, according to the synoptic gospels, it was on the Thursday before he died that Jesus prayed for the church, washed his disciples' feet, served a meal of bread and wine that signified his death, and was betrayed. Thus all Thursdays can be seen as sanctified by the Spirit of Christ.

What about all those calendars that begin the week with Monday? Don't use them. Keep Sunday as the first day of the week. On your devices and on your calendars at home and in the parish, continue to organize Christian life as always beginning on Sunday, when we join with the baptized community on that first day to praise Christ's resurrection and to begin time anew in the Spirit. The dominant culture, in which each week opens with Monday's workday and closes with "the weekend," will not support our efforts to value each Sunday as the renewal of all things, giving purpose to our days and meaning to our death. But a weekly scriptural reinsertion of the community into the proclamation of the death and resurrection of Christ will assist us in this baptismal grounding.

Principle 1 in wider context

The Christian meeting on Sunday is an example of the endless human practice of ritualizing, of assembling for repetitive, communal, symbolic activities. Humans are a ritualizing species,[18] and rituals lend order to our lives: "Each ritual is a repeated, coherently structured, and unified aspect of our experience. In performing [rituals], we give structure and significance to our activities, minimizing chaos and disparity in our actions."[19] There is no human society on record that did not rely on rituals to form coherent and cooperative living. Ancient Babylon presents us with an early example of a society that scheduled a day to hold markets for buying and selling produce. Perhaps it was the seven "movable planets," those visible heavenly bodies thought to govern human destiny, that determined the week, one day of which was designated for marketing. By thus keeping the week, society would find itself following the patterns of the universe itself. Our society continues to keep weekly rituals, whether sabbath for observant Jews or Monday night football for countless Americans.

One goal of ritual gatherings is to situate the individual within the cosmos. Thus the late twentieth century witnessed the revival of solstice festivals: by celebrating the return of the sun, the community attends to the ecological cosmic order. Rituals also situate the individual within the history of the community, revitalizing memory and reactivating joint action. To continuously reinsert the individual into the communal, governments encourage annual festivals and identity organizations celebrate their founder's birthday. Cultural anthropologists suggest that, given the relative weakness of the lone individual, early cultures relied on communal bonding for survival. Indeed, only because communal ritual was so valuable can we make any sense of, for example, the immense amount of effort that was required for the construction of a Stonehenge or for the ceremonies in which ecstatic experiences were valued.[20] Rituals also celebrate the uniqueness of the individual within the community. In our time, birthday parties and rites of passage such as weddings have introduced "save the date" announcements, as the whole community is asked to set aside time for rituals that focus on the few.

Humans rely on rituals to suggest a past and a future to their days and years.

Rituals do not encourage imaginative time-travel back into the past. Rather, the past event is brought into the present and shaped by a contemporary pattern of celebration. In the United States, Thanksgiving is the most-observed communal ritual, able to blend nationalism, religion, ethnicity, and family in one festive gesture of sharing symbolic foods. Thus arises the unrest when some family members refuse to eat the foods on the traditional menu: the communal ritual is challenged. However, we do not don seventeenth-century costumes for the feast, for the past is continually reconfigured to fit into the present.

Despite the emphasis over the last five centuries in the West on the autonomy of the individual, that human individual is always set within a community.

Like tattoos, the community's rituals—their repeated symbolic communal activities—mark time, energy, and even one's very body as connected with others. Whether that connection is established by one's birth into an ethnic group or is personally chosen for private reasons, humans rely on rituals to suggest a past and a future to their days and years. It misunderstands how humans function to imagine that we could live profoundly without participation in some communal rituals. Even secular nations designate some annual holidays, as testimony to the value of such ritualizing for the good of the whole. Recent sociological studies suggest that innovations in ritual are primary catalysts for personal and communal identity movements: because rituals demonstrate and enact meaning, change in ritual is of high significance.[21] The world's religions expect at least some level of loyal participation in their regularly recurring rituals, for it is not easy or automatic for individuals to adhere to the values of their communities of choice without such dedicated participation. This volume deals with the Christian Sunday, one such communal ritual of formation and support.

Examples of principle 1

Second Sunday of Easter (RCL, LM), Years A, B, C

In the three-year lectionaries, each of the more than two hundred sets of readings (the number depends on what and how you count) attempts to reinsert the baptized community into the meaning of the death and resurrection of Christ. One clear example occurs on the first Sunday after Easter Day, the second Sunday of the season, "Easter" being designated not as a single day but as fifty days long. John 20:19-31 has been deemed so significant that it is appointed for all three years.

In the gospel reading on the second Sunday of Easter, the risen Christ appears among the gathered disciples both on the day of the resurrection and also a week later. The risen Christ shows his wounds, for the resurrection testifies to, rather than obliterates, his sufferings and death. Although we, assembled for the Sunday ritual, were not present at the empty tomb, we are those who gather a week later. In holding the communion bread, we are those who have touched the body of Christ, along with Thomas. This gospel reading includes the description of Christ greeting his disciples with peace, and it is this biblical passage that has become ritualized in the Sunday handshake or kiss of peace. In true ritual fashion, the ancient story has been brought into the current time, the past working its power in the present.

For the first reading on Easter 2, although the RCL and the LM appoint different versification of the readings, both begin the six weeks of Eastertide selections with texts from the Acts of the Apostles. Acts, the second volume of Luke, attests that the Spirit of Christ's preaching, ministry, and resurrection continues in the experience of the church. Apostolic sermons summarize the story of Jesus, and both in the lives of named individuals and in the experience of the community as a whole, believers live out the resurrection in extraordinary ways. Thus Easter continues through the first century and into our time.

For the second reading in all three years of the Easter season, the lectionary turns to late first-century writings that urge the community to faithfulness. In year A, the lectionary begins a semicontinuous reading through the epistle of 1 Peter. This letter states that the community of the resurrection will find it extremely difficult to live their rebirth in Christ in this world, and the author prays for the community to be strong even in the face of persecution. For the second reading in year B, the lectionary begins a semicontinuous reading through 1 John, an essay that urges the community to live in love and to maintain the truth of the gospel teachings. The author warns the community to beware of distorted versions of the message of Christ that would result in a loss of love within the community. For the second reading in year C, the lectionary turns to a semicontinuous reading of the book of Revelation, an apocalyptic writing that anticipates the ultimate victory of Christ and his church over the current, reigning empire of evil. In selecting passages from the book of Revelation, the lectionaries omit all the horrific descriptions of violent conflict that are part of the seer's visions, and instead focus on the praises of the gathered people at the end of time. The faithful affirm that not Darius the Great, nor the Roman emperor, but the risen Christ is the king of kings, and that the body of Christ, gathered on Sunday, is in some way already that throng victorious over sin and death.

Thus this lectionary family gathers believers on the second Sunday of Easter, as well as for all the subsequent weeks of Easter's fifty days, around and into scriptural readings that enact the meaning of the Sunday ritual by proclaiming the ongoing reality of the Spirit of the risen Christ. Each week the baptized assembly comes deeper into the Easter event, which not only happened way back then, but occurs every single Sunday during worship.

Proper 4 (RCL) / Ninth Sunday in Ordinary Time (LM), Year B

Readings on other Sundays during the three years expand Christian awareness of the meaning of the resurrection. On this Sunday the gospel reading, Mark 2:23—3:6, narrates one of Jesus' healing miracles and deals with differences between the Jewish ritual of sabbath and the Christian Sunday meeting. Historically there have been times and places in which church practice, or even civil law, required Sunday to be a day of rest from most work and from much play.[22] But according to this Markan passage, Jesus, the apocalyptic Son of Man, is himself the meaning of the holy day. As background to the gospel reading, the first reading in the RCL* and the LM, Deuteronomy 5:12-15, proclaims the meaning of the Israelite sabbath as a rest in reminder of freedom from slavery: Christians see Sunday as the day to celebrate our release from slavery to evil. In the RCL+, the first reading is 1 Samuel 3:1-10, the narrative of the boy Samuel hearing the voice of God in the temple. Christians understand that on Sunday we are now in "the temple," residing in the body of Christ. The second reading, 2 Corinthians 4:5-12 in the RCL and 2 Corinthians 4:6-11 in the LM, is itself a proclamation of the death and resurrection of Christ. Our current sufferings are embodiments of the death of Christ, but with Christ as our risen Lord, we are enlivened with divine light.

Proper 23 (RCL) / Twenty-eighth Sunday in Ordinary Time (LM), Year A

We can test the principle that every Sunday is Easter by looking at a lectionary set that includes the surprisingly harsh parable in Matthew 22:1-14. Taken from a gospel that was written in about the year 80 mainly for Jewish Christians, the parable ascribed to Jesus tells about a banquet that the king hosts to celebrate his son's wedding. Many of the invited send their regrets, so the king fills his hall with "both good and bad" people invited in from the streets. But one guest who is not wearing a wedding robe gets thrown out into "the outer darkness, where there will be weeping and gnashing of teeth."

. . . .

The three readings—a veritable trinity—collaborate to speak of the Spirit of the risen Christ within the Sunday assembly.

. . . .

How can this disturbing parable be proclaiming the resurrection? Several centuries of biblical studies have taught that no parable or narrative episode ought to stand alone, isolated from the gospel from which it was excerpted. Each part takes its meaning from the whole. Hearing this parable, the baptized community knows that although it may not have been on the initial guest list, on this Sunday—thanks to the resurrection of Jesus Christ—it is dining at God's table of mercy. Today we wear our baptismal robes and share in the supper of the kingdom.

For their first readings on this Sunday, the lectionary variants all cite passages that include the biblical image of the mountain as the dwelling of God. In the poem from Isaiah 25 (RCL*, LM), God has set out a feast on a mountain, and there will destroy death forever. And so as Christians we think of Golgotha, where we gladly receive salvation. Those who use RCL+ hear from Exodus 32 the story of the Israelites making for themselves a golden calf to worship. Moses, still up on the mountain, pleads with God to grant the people forgiveness. Mercy is on and from the mountain of God. In the second reading of the day from Philippians 4, Paul confirms the believers in the joy of the risen Christ. The Lord is near; the peace of God will guard their lives. God will fully supply whatever they need. This lectionary set illustrates the intention of the three-year lectionaries that the gospel reading seek biblical company: the three readings—a veritable trinity—collaborate to speak of the Spirit of the risen Christ within the Sunday assembly.

Often the victory of Christ over sin and death is heard in the gospel reading, but sometimes the gospel passage is helped by the first and second readings in proclaiming its Easter message.

As Martin Kähler wrote over a century ago, "The reason we commune with the Jesus of our Gospels is because . . . he who once walked on earth and now is exalted is the incarnate Word of God, the image of the invisible God—because he is for us God revealed."[23] It is this Word of God, this risen Christ, that the lectionary proclaims, Sunday after Sunday.

NOTES

1   See Willy Rordorf, *Sunday: The History of the Day of Rest and Worship in the Earliest Centuries of the Christian Church* (Philadelphia: Westminster, 1968), 193-215. Also see Philip A. Harland, *Associations, Synagogues, and Congregations: Claiming a Place in Ancient Mediterranean Society* (Minneapolis: Fortress, 2003), 182.

2   For a succinct account of this development, see Craig Harline, *Sunday: A History of the First Day from Babylonia to the Super Bowl* (New York: Doubleday, 2007), 1-25.

3   Harline, *Sunday*, 24-25.

4   For the roots of Sunday in the Easter event, see Rordorf, *Sunday*, 215-37. Also Andrew B. McGowan, *Ancient Christian Worship: Early Church Practices in Social, Historical, and Theological Perspective* (Grand Rapids, MI: Baker Academic, 2014), 229-37.

5   Harline, *Sunday*, 14.

6   See Risto Uro, *Ritual and Christian Beginnings: A Socio-Cognitive Analysis* (Oxford, UK: Oxford University Press, 2016), for a discussion of the primary role played by ritual practices toward the rapid rise of Christianity.

7   Rordorf, *Sunday*, 291.

8   This translation of Justin is taken from Gordon W. Lathrop, *Central Things: Worship in Word and Sacrament* (Minneapolis: Augsburg Fortress, 2005), 79.

9   Lee Martin McDonald, *Formation of the Bible: The Story of the Church's Canon* (Peabody, MA: Hendrickson, 2012), 87-93.

10 See, for example, Thomas G. Bandy, *Introducing the Uncommon Lectionary: Opening the Bible to Seekers and Disciples* (Nashville: Abingdon, 2006), 144-60.

11 See, for example, the Narrative Lectionary, www.workingpreacher.org.

12 Donald B. Kraybill, Steven M. Nolt, and David L. Weaver-Zercher, *The Amish Way: Patient Faith in a Perilous World* (San Francisco: Jossey-Bass, 2010), 205-7.

13 *Evangelical Lutheran Worship, Leaders Desk Edition* (Minneapolis: Augsburg Fortress, 2006), 180, passim.

14 Gail R. O'Day and Charles Hackett, *Preaching the Revised Common Lectionary: A Guide* (Nashville: Abingdon, 2007), xi.

15 O'Day and Hackett, *Preaching the Revised Common Lectionary*, xii, xiii.

16 See Raymond E. Brown, *Christ in the Gospels of the Liturgical Year*, expanded ed. (Collegeville, MN: Liturgical Press, 2008), 43-142.

17 Martin Kähler, *The So-Called Historical Jesus and the Historic, Biblical Christ* [1896], trans. Carl E. Braaten (Philadelphia: Fortress, 1964), 80, n. 11.

18 See Roy A. Rappaport, *Ritual and Religion in the Making of Humanity* (Cambridge, UK: Cambridge University Press, 1999), 138.

19 George Lakoff and Mark Johnson, *Metaphors We Live By* (Chicago: University of Chicago Press, 2003), 233-34.

20 Brian Hayden, *Shamans, Sorcerers, and Saints: A Prehistory of Religion* (Washington: Smithsonian Books, 2003).

21 Uro, *Ritual and Christian Beginnings*, 73-75.

22 Harline, *Sunday*, 19-22, 28-32.

23 Kähler, *The So-Called Historical Jesus*, 60-61.

Principle 2

ABOUT THE FOUR
DISTINCTIVE GOSPELS

Since many have undertaken to set down an orderly account of the events that have been fulfilled among us, just as they were handed on to us by those who from the beginning were eyewitnesses and servants of the word, I too decided, after investigating everything carefully from the very first, to write an orderly account for you, most excellent Theophilus, so that you may know the truth concerning the things about which you have been instructed.

Luke 1:1-4

. . . .

2 Many Christians agree that a passage from a gospel is the primary reading on each Sunday and festival. Because the four gospels narrate the story of Jesus Christ in different ways, the three-year lectionaries appoint readings from all four.

Principle 2 in the lectionary

Given the opening verses in the Gospel according to Luke, it is surprising that countless Christians have been taught that the Bible was dictated verbatim by the Holy Spirit to those writers who functioned as God's amanuenses. The passage above, from Luke 1, describes first the eyewitnesses to the ministry of Christ—now often referred to as the "Jesus movement"—who spoke their testimony to a second generation; this second generation of believers began to compose interpretive narratives of Christ, after which the author of this gospel undertook personal study of the emerging religious tradition. Thus in the book we call Luke we encounter not automatic writing, but something like a dissertation with a clear thesis. A twenty-first-century consensus of biblical scholars reckons the four gospels to have been crafted by at least four different authors over the years 70 to perhaps 100. This widespread theory corresponds with the data cited at the outset of Luke that describes a text written by a believer two to three generations after the ministry, death, and resurrection of Jesus.[1]

. . . .

The Bible is not a set of railroad tracks, but a complex tree, and the narration of Jesus' life has four primary branches.

. . . .

In some situations, it is best if there is only a single testimony concerning the deceased: for example, one undisputed will that is attested to by reliable witnesses. In the second century, a Syrian Christian named Tatian, a student of Justin, sought just such a single text recording the life and meaning of Jesus Christ. Faced, however, with four gospels, all of which were commonly cited and receiving ecclesial authority, Tatian edited the four into a single narrative called the Diatessaron. In this way, he was able to delete not only doublets but, potentially more embarrassing for the emerging church, contradictions of fact and interpretation, of which the four gospels present many examples. Not since the fifth century have any churches used the Diatessaron in public worship. However, the widespread phenomenon of children's Bibles may have a similar lasting influence on adult knowledge about the actual Bible.[2] Other biblical compilations in our time are the many popular movies that purport to depict the life of Jesus, which, while cementing vivid images into viewers' memories, have done so with considerable fabrication about and around the biblical record.[3] One of many challenges for any lectionary is to carry the faithful beyond childhood and into an adult reception of God's word.

Tatian's efforts were opposed and his preference for a single text defeated in part by Irenaeus, bishop of Lyons. Irenaeus wrote of the absolute need for the church to maintain each of the four gospels separately, for he judged that the differences they presented offered complementary theologies that were necessary for the fullness of proclamation of God's word. Indeed, one danger with self-generated lectionaries is that one's favorite gospel or one's preferred story line may take precedence over the others. Although Irenaeus's comparison of the four gospels to "the four zones of the world in which we live, and four principal winds" is not to our taste, his primary argument remains relevant: that a partial focus on perhaps only one of the gospels would result in heretical beliefs. Irenaeus likened these four witnesses to the four living creatures that appear in Ezekiel's vision and reappear in Revelation 4:6b-9 surrounding the throne and the Lamb. Matthew has been likened to the winged man, to correspond with the gospel's opening genealogy; Mark as the lion, to reflect the reference from Isaiah concerning Jesus' prophetic power; Luke as the ox, to recall the narrative of the priest Zechariah's offerings in the temple; and John as the eagle, who soars highest and sees farthest with the Spirit who hovers over the church.[4]

The four gospels are not the only canonical texts that engage in conversation, if not controversy, with other biblical books: The Torah promulgates the patriarchal preference for the eldest son, yet Seth, Isaac, Jacob, and David are not eldest sons. The book of Nehemiah condemns the marriages of Jews with non-Jews, while the book of Ruth lauds a Moabite woman as the great-grandmother of King David. Worship in the temple is mandated by God, while Amos claims that God rejects the people's religious rituals. Paul and James have debated with one another now for two thousand years. The Bible is not a set of railroad tracks, but a complex tree, and the narration of Jesus' life has four primary branches—whether that makes proclamation easy for the church or not.

The differences between the four gospels challenge the habit of a strict literalist reading of the New Testament. When printed Bibles became affordable for the laity and individual meditation on biblical texts became a recommended daily discipline, literalist reading of the scriptures became commonplace. Each devout believer could read narratives about Jesus without any recourse to original languages, translation theory, comparative textual study, and historical knowledge of biblical times. A reader's piety, aided by editions of the Bible in which Jesus' words were printed in red, would not be questioned by the learned study undertaken by others. What is intriguing about a literalist reading of the Bible is that it honors a late medieval Western value—that relatively uneducated people ought to be able to read—but refuses to incorporate the more recent development of critical interpretive skills. It is instructive that the earliest eighteenth-century novels were presented as if they were factual accounts of real people, there being little societal appreciation of imaginative texts that relied on a discriminating reader for intelligent reception.

To replace such popular literalism with the discoveries of several centuries of faithful Christian scholarship, churches will welcome a lectionary that does not hide the variations in the scriptural records. When the lectionary's choices make clear, for example, that the synoptic gospels describe Jesus' last supper as the Passover meal while the Gospel according to John fixes Jesus' death during the slaughter of the Passover lambs, the notion that biblical texts are to be interpreted literally—and a consequent religious disillusionment when such a reading shows itself to be impossible to maintain—is corrected by catechesis concerning the different theologies that are at work in the four evangelists.

In our time, many people also mistake the gospels for a genre they know better: the biography. However, the four gospels show little interest in the kinds of data that contemporary biographies present—precise details of life events and, even more so, proposed psychological explanations for human actions. Rather, the gospels are interpretive records of the faith of early churches, and since the second century, the majority judgment in the churches has been that proclaiming four such testimonies is better than relying on one. In Christianity, what was canonized as scripture is the diversity of biblical conversation, accessed in a multitude of translations. The hope that all four gospels will proclaim their unique Christology to all the faithful gathered for worship has been masterfully met by the three-year lectionaries. Let us now consider each of the four gospels in order. We begin with the lectionary's linchpin, the Gospel according to John.

The Gospel according to John is not the easiest of the four to understand. Indeed, a simple-minded religion is an unlikely candidate to withstand centuries of questions, challenges, conflicts, and sorrows. The fourth gospel is, however, the one that contributed most to the church's subsequent development of the theology of Christ, articulating what has been termed "the highest Christology" in the New Testament. The description of the second person of the Trinity in the Nicene Creed as the one "eternally begotten of the Father, God from God, Light from Light" reflects language found in John. Its opening chapter exemplifies this focus on the identity of Jesus as the Word, the light of all, the Lamb of God, the Son of God, Rabbi, the Messiah, the son of Joseph from Nazareth, King of Israel, and the Son of Man. In later chapters, this gospel describes Jesus as the temple; the bridegroom; living water; the bread from heaven; not only the shepherd, but also the gate of the sheepfold; the resurrection and the life; the true vine; the King of the Jews; and, finally, "my Lord and my God." As Jesus says of himself in John 8:58, "Before Abraham was, I am," and they began to stone him for having claimed identity with God, the great I AM. Written probably in the late first or early second century, this gospel is the result of several decades of theological reflection on Christ, which, while utilizing Greco-Roman philosophical and poetic imagery, distances the churches both from Jewish religious beliefs and from an emerging Gnostic distortion of God's creation. To accomplish this, the gospel relishes the "figures of speech" (John 16:25) that are deemed necessary in articulating the mystery of the God incarnate in Jesus and in expressing the paradoxical faith that through an execution God has given life to the world. The fourth gospel prods our thought and inspires our imagination.

The role that the Gospel according to John played in Christian theology is evident in its placement over the three years of the lectionaries. Were Christians to attend worship only on the highest festivals—Christmas

Day, Maundy Thursday, Good Friday, Easter Vigil or Easter Day, and Pentecost—they would hear the gospel solely from John. The gospel readings also come from John on sixteen of the eighteen Sundays of the fifty days of Easter over the course of the three-year cycle, on over half of the Sundays of Lent, and on five weeks in the summertime in year B. This volume will examine some of these lectionary choices, as well as the Johannine statements about "the Jews" that many Christians find so distressing.

Circling around the central John are the three synoptic gospels, which the lectionary appoints in canonical order.

In year A the lectionary reads semicontinuously through Matthew. Although it includes much material from the Gospel according to Mark, Matthew adds much that is unique. Written in about the year 80, the Gospel according to Matthew assumes a largely Jewish readership; Jesus is likened to Moses and his teachings to the Torah. The genealogy of Jesus in Matthew 1 begins with Jewish patriarch Abraham. Jesus fulfills the promises made to the prophets; he is the Messiah born of the Davidic line. Probably in respect to Jewish sensibilities concerning the name of God, the author of Matthew amended the earlier phrase "the kingdom of God" into "the kingdom of heaven." In Matthew 12:30 we see the Matthean attention to the situation of a persecuted community: "Whoever is not with me is against me." The repeated call to obedience within the community of the faithful would sound familiar to practicing Jews, while the sometimes harsh parables of the kingdom in chapters 21–25 reflect the belief that God, the judge of all, requires that believers live an ethical life. Soon God will bring about the eschaton— another reprise of Jewish beliefs. "Be perfect," we read in Matthew 5:48.

In year B the lectionary reads semicontinuously through the Gospel according to Mark. It is judged by a consensus of scholars to be the earliest gospel, written perhaps in the year 70, thus one to two generations after the ministry of Jesus. The Gospel according to Mark, which describes the Messiah as the power of God hidden from the world, is addressed to those early Christians who are themselves hidden from the wider world. That God was active in Jesus is revealed in the empty tomb; to see the risen Christ, the community is to meet together, read these words, and share the meal of his death. Repeatedly the original disciples had misunderstood Jesus, although some women—socially hidden persons—did better than many of the men at faithfulness to the message of the cross. All are fervently awaiting the eschaton. Christ, risen from death, will come again, but persecution and misery of many kinds will precede the end. So in Mark 13:37 Jesus says, "Keep awake."

In year C, the lectionary reads semicontinuously through the Gospel according to Luke. This last of the synoptic gospels quotes much of Mark and adds considerable unique material. Written in perhaps 90 for a largely Gentile readership, the Gospel according to Luke no longer anticipates an imminent eschaton. Rather, the author addresses a community that wants to normalize the emerging religion, hoping to survive and to thrive in the whole of the Roman Empire. In Luke 3, the genealogy of Jesus heads back to Adam, who is the primordial human, rather than the Jewish patriarch. "Whoever is not against you is for you," is advice given in Luke 9:50. It is safe to say that the Gospel according to Luke is the most beloved of gospels, given its many engaging narratives, its attention to Mary, its inclusion of early Christian song texts, and its memorable and comforting parables. Its author was indeed a talented writer. The quality repeatedly stressed in the ministry of Jesus is his divine forgiveness. This trait must be practiced also in and by the religious community, which experiences the presence of the risen Christ at its regular communal meals. To follow Christ and his apostles, "be merciful," we read in Luke 6:36.

"Be perfect." "Keep awake." "Be merciful." "I AM." In Matthew, Jesus is the new Moses; in Mark, Jesus is the hidden Messiah; in Luke, Jesus is the universal Savior; in John, Jesus is God. In the three-year lectionaries, we sit at the feet of each gospel, attending to its unique depiction of Christ and its specific messages to Christian communities.[5] The churches can be grateful that this lectionary family honors the Spirit of God alive also in the work of scholars who provide assistance to our reading of these first-century witnesses to faith in Christ.

Principle 2 in wider context

Although our society has become accustomed to the cacophony created by a diversity of voices, countless humans have lived and died in small homogeneous hamlets without either involvement with or even knowledge of other communities filled with people who spoke foreign languages, maintained alien rites of passage, worshiped different deities, and enforced unheard-of ethical systems. Such a narrow existence perhaps had its advantages. When in our time this type of uniform living is lauded, sometimes without recourse to much historical data about what such life was genuinely like, the notion is that one way, one religion, one moral pattern made life easier than is granted to nearly all twenty-first-century people, who not only permit an alien life pattern to exist among their neighbors—they marry into it. In 1754, Gottlieb Mittelberger, a German visitor, wrote about his encounters in colonial Pennsylvania:

> The colony of Pennsylvania possesses great liberties above all other English colonies, inasmuch as all religious sects are tolerated there. We find there Lutherans, Reformed, Catholics, Quakers, Mennonites or Anabaptists, Herrnhutters or Moravian Brethren, Pietists, Seventh Day Baptists, Dunkers, Presbyterians, Newborn, Free-masons, Separatists, Freethinkers, Jews, Mohammedans, Pagans, Negroes and Indians. But there are many hundred unbaptized souls there who do not even wish to be baptized. In one house and one family, 4, 5, and even 6 sects may be found.[6]

Distressed by such communal diversity, Mittelberger returned to his own homogeneous European community.

The twenty-first century certainly has its share of persons who, like Mittelberger, find it difficult to tolerate diversity. Mittelberger wanted his neighbors to mirror himself, and when this was not the case, he felt threatened. We witness an alarming rise of small, fearful, sometimes militant groups who maintain strict separation from others, unable to countenance systems that diverge from their own. One voice enjoys the right of expression. Such groups may be well armed, either for protection or for conquest. Ambiguity threatens the single system, and thus it is forbidden. In ethnic groups, isolation is desirable. In some nation-states, only the one way is legal. In religion, this attitude sometimes takes the form of preference for a univocal voice, a community gladly following the voice of a single leader. Only one narrow message is deemed sacred. Even if the Bible is cited as the source of the single voice, history has shown an astonishing array of small communities in which one leader maintains absolute tyrannical authority over others, at least some of whom willingly receive only that voice as if channeling words from God.

This consideration of those who in our time hanker after univocality is not meant to imply that the use of other lectionaries encourages totalitarian domination of the many by the one. However, it might suggest that wherever we can, we ought to make choices that replace a restricted univocality with the actual heterogeneous situation of human living. People are urged to consult more than one source of news, to get a second opinion before major surgery, to welcome a diversity of voices, and to find their security in a community of wide tolerance characterized by critical thinking.

Examples of principle 2

Most children's Bibles include one appealing story about the birth of Jesus that focuses on the crèche. In the stable the ox and the ass are attending the baby: perhaps the parent knows that those animals come from Isaiah 1:3, in which the prophet condemns the people for their disregard of God, although even the farm animals recognize their owner, their "master's crib." Children's Bibles usually include both the shepherds and the magi, generally depicted as kings.

But to proclaim the incarnation, the three-year lectionaries go beyond this conflation of Matthew and Luke. Maintaining a tradition in the Western church that the celebration of the birth of Christ lasts not twenty-four hours but twelve days, the lectionaries envision the Christmas season as lasting from December 25 up to Epiphany, January 6. The season includes readings from three of the gospels—John, Luke, and Matthew—that attend to Jesus' birth. On Epiphany the lectionary appoints a story connected with Jesus' birth from Matthew, and in the middle of June we hear from Mark. Thus the three-year lectionaries honor the scriptural diversity of four voices, each gospel speaking of the origins of Jesus.

The Nativity of the Lord, Christmas Day (RCL, LM), Years A, B, C

The three-year lectionaries provide three different sets of biblical readings for what we colloquially call "Christmas." The lectionary's guidelines indicate that for the worship that is held on mid- to late morning on December 25, the readings surrounding John 1 are the appropriate choice—this despite the fact that worship on what we call Christmas Eve or "Midnight Mass" is attended by far more people than is the liturgy on Christmas Day. It is interesting that at Easter the reverse is true: the Sunday mid-morning liturgy on Easter Day is more popular than is the festal service of the Easter Vigil held on Saturday night. Let this incongruity about attendance stand for the various ways that the intention of the lectionary is not always the direction taken by worshiping communities.

The appointed gospel reading for Christmas Day is John 1:1-14 (RCL) or 1:1-18 (LM), the prologue to the Gospel according to John. This poem is generally understood to have been a Christological hymn sung by the Johannine community, into which an editor of the gospel has inserted several explanatory passages (vv. 6-9, 12b-13, 15).[7] In much of the Roman Empire, the days surrounding December 25 were marked as the festival of *Natalis solis invicti*, the birthday of the unconquered sun, a celebration that had carried into the first century the ancient celebration of the winter solstice in the Northern Hemisphere. This cultural celebration of new life made the Christian hymn of John 1 especially appropriate. (Verse 5 praises Christ the Word as the light that the darkness cannot overcome.) By tying this hymn to the winter solstice, the church in the Northern Hemisphere was able to offer a seasonally appropriate Christianized description of life on earth. Recently, some Christians in the Southern Hemisphere have advocated a reversal of the liturgical year, so that their Christmas would occur near to their winter solstice.

Rather than narrating any stories of Jesus' birth, the fourth gospel proclaims the theology of the incarnation: Jesus is the Word of God, who existed with God since before the beginning of time. Just as the Word created the world "in the beginning," so now the Word revealed by God brings about the new creation, in which divine love will transform us all into children of God. The vocabulary in the prologue—*Word, life, light, world, flesh, glory, love*— functions as a kind of table of contents for the whole gospel. These terms have resonance in both Jewish religious tradition and contemporary Greek philosophical discussion, and so the fourth evangelist hopes to proclaim the meaning of the gospel to the whole culture. The primary title of Christ, "the Word," has several referents: the way the Hebrew scriptures depict God as the one who spoke creation into being and who continually communicates with humankind; the way Greek thought spoke about the mind of God; the commitment of early Christians to speak of Christ to the whole world; and the actual situation of a weekly gathered community of faith whose members share in that Word with one another.

In the first reading that accompanies John 1—Isaiah 52:7-10—is the promise that the exiles will return to their homeland; that God, coming in majesty, will reside once again with the people; and that all the earth will see this "salvation of our God." The second reading is an excerpt from Hebrews 1, which, in speaking of the person of Christ, situates the Son at the very creation of the world. Thus in this set of readings for Christmas Day, Christ is the hero conquering the power of Babylon, the heir of God's power, the light of the darkened earth, and the word of salvation to the whole world. Inspired by these Johannine readings about divine power and the transformation of all things, the lectionaries proclaim the Christmas paradox that the infant in the parish's crèche and sung in Christmas carols is in fact the Savior who came to die, the Son of the triune God.

The Nativity of the Lord, Christmas Eve (RCL, LM), Years A, B, C

The gospel reading appointed for Christmas Eve is Luke 2:1-14. The beloved narrative contains several themes that are important to this evangelist, all of which are helpful in receiving this narrative as other than "a charming memory."[8] First, it is instructive that the Christian author of the late first century can give credit to the Roman emperor for bringing about God's will, since thanks to the census (which is not attested to by any secular sources), the child Jesus will be born in Bethlehem. This proclaims Jesus as descended from the house of David and, so, the inheritor of the monarchy and of the mission to enact God's will. The reading includes concrete first-century historical details: the Roman emperor, the governor of Syria, and the hometown of Joseph are all named. It is as if this history provides a reality base over which the angels will sing of peace on earth.

A second Lukan focus is the adoration of the shepherds. David was honored as originally a shepherd, but in the first century in the lands around Jerusalem, shepherds, far from our sentimental imaginings, were an underclass, considered by devout Jews to be ritually unclean. Yet they serve the evangelist as examples of the poor to whom Christ comes and whom he joins at table. Another emphasis in the Christmas narrative is specific detail about Mary, one of the many women throughout the gospel and Acts whom this author describes as indispensable to the early Christian community.

The first reading that complements Luke 2, the oracle in Isaiah 9:2-7 (RCL) and Isaiah 9:1-6 (LM), opens with the imagery of light and promises that God will keep covenant with the people, eventually sending them an ideal monarch who will establish a reign of justice. The second reading, Titus 2:11-14, is a late-first-century summary of the Christian faith: the grace of God has appeared, here in the worshiping community gathered for word and sacrament. The original Greek text makes clear in verse 13 that "our great God and Savior" is the one Jesus Christ. Thus this reading also grants the Lukan infant as high an identification as possible: this Jesus is our great God, given for us.

Epiphany of the Lord (RCL, LM), Years A, B, C

The Gospel according to Matthew describes the birth of Jesus so differently from Luke's gospel that the church can be lauded for its ingenuity in fitting the two together. Matthew's account of the role Joseph plays in the drama provides the gospel reading for the fourth Sunday of Advent in year A, and the treasured narrative about the coming of the magi, told in Matthew 2:1-12, serves the church for the festival of the Epiphany. Epiphany follows after the twelve days of Christmas and, especially in the Eastern church, is celebrated as a high feast and baptismal festival. In much of southern Europe, Epiphany is the day of annual gift-giving, as if Christians are mimicking the gesture of the magi's gifts to Jesus. Some contemporary churches transfer the festival from January 6 to the nearest Sunday, in order to give it sufficient attention in our secularized society.

The story of the magi includes many of the themes in the Gospel according to Matthew.[9] This infancy narrative of Jesus the Messiah, the king of the Jews, anticipates the language used to describe the execution of Jesus in Matthew 26–27. Matthew's birth narrative focuses on the roles of important men: Joseph, King Herod, the chief priests and scribes, the magi. Being king of the Jews, Jesus is born in Bethlehem in Judea—that is, in Jewish territory. The Gentiles receive the revelation of the Messiah through nature, by means of the star in the sky, but the author hopes that the Jewish audience sees the connection with the story of Balaam in Numbers 22–24, in which "a star shall come out of Jacob" (24:17). That these stories of Jesus' early life function as literary prefaces to the main point of the gospels—the death and resurrection of Christ—is clear here: in the Matthean narrative, King Herod threatens the life of the Messiah, and although he does not succeed at this time, a later Herod does. The magi, probably astrologers, perhaps including both men and women, present symbolic gifts that a Jew might recognize from the psalms—gold, to honor Jesus as a king, and frankincense, to worship his divinity—as well as myrrh, to anticipate his death.

On Christmas Eve, we hear from first Isaiah; on Christmas Day, from second Isaiah; and now on Epiphany, from third Isaiah. The poem in 60:1-6 sings out Jerusalem's joy at the arrival of God's light. The light shines not only on the Jews, but also on distant nations. The second reading that accompanies the story of the magi is from Ephesians 3, a late-first-century writing that emphasizes Christ's welcome to the Gentiles. Jesus, the Messiah, is the revelation of God's mystery shown also to the Gentiles, and we think of the magi, as well as of most of those gathered in our own Christian assemblies.

Proper 5 (RCL*) / Tenth Sunday in Ordinary Time (LM), Year B

And how does this lectionary that listens to all four of the evangelists hear a word concerning Jesus' birth from the Gospel according to Mark? This earliest gospel includes no comment about nor stories narrating the birth of Jesus. If this evangelist had heard such stories, they were afforded no value. For this evangelist, the time is short, the end is coming: what matters is not Jesus' birth but rather his ministry, passion, death, and resurrection. Yet the lectionary does include a significant reference to Jesus' family, Mark 3:20-35, appointed not at Christmas time, but rather during June in year B (followed by a parallel four weeks later from Mark 6:1-13).

* *

With this lectionary, worshipers hear all four gospels, each with its distinctive resonance on who Jesus is and how the Christian community is to live.

* *

"[Jesus] went home," begins the excerpt, where he engaged in a debate with both family members and religious authorities concerning his mental health. The suggestion that he is possessed by a demon introduces a discussion of Jesus as exorcist, as one who with the power of God is overcoming the reign of Satan. Here we encounter a primary theme of this first gospel: through Jesus, God is freeing the world from its subjection to evil. "Then his mother and his brothers came," joining with others who were questioning Jesus' sanity.

In this story the evangelist juxtaposes Jesus' birth family, for whom the gospel shows almost no interest, with what can be called the Christian "fictive family." Those who believe in Jesus and who do the will of God are what interests this evangelist. Worshipers gathered around his word are Jesus' "brother and sister and mother," and this family stands together against the power of Satan. This replacement of a natural family with the family of the baptized fits with the actual historical situation of the church as this first evangelist experienced it: it was not entire families that were converted, and so individuals came to see other believers as the family that mattered. In one of the many similarities between the gospels of Mark and John, the fundamental truth of the incarnation is the making of believers into children of God.

The first reading that accompanies this Markan narrative is Genesis 3:8-15 (RCL*) or Genesis 3:9-15 (LM), in which God curses the evil that is represented by the serpent. The lectionary sets this section of the story of the human fall next to the Markan discussion of Satan because Christians have seen in the Genesis tale a picture of the power of Satan, the power that Christ is alive to conquer. The second reading on this Sunday, as the lectionary reads semicontinuously through New Testament epistles, is 2 Corinthians 4:13—5:1. This excerpt contrasts our outer with our inner nature, what is temporary with what is eternal, our earthly dwelling with the house of God. On the Sunday of Mark 3, what is temporary—for one thing, our natural family—is replaced by the family created by faith in Jesus as Messiah.

So it is that with this lectionary, worshipers hear all four gospels, each with its distinctive resonance on who Jesus is and how the Christian community is to live. Meditating on the incarnation of Christ, we encounter Luke's appealing narrative of good news for the poor, John's poetic theology of the cosmic Christ, Matthew's description of the kingship of Jesus, and Mark's call to live as the family of God. We receive all four witnesses. Whichever is our favorite is there, enhanced by those that perhaps we would not voluntarily choose.

NOTES

1   In our time, Luke's introductory data must contend with the well-known lyrics in the 1970 rock opera *Jesus Christ Superstar*: at the last supper the disciples sing that when they retire, they will write the gospels.

2   So it is that I urge care in selecting children's Bibles. My favorite children's Bible is written in prose that reflects the scriptural text, does not introduce fantasy figures, includes seven New Testament stories beyond Pentecost, and, with one illustration per story, never depicts God as an old man. See *The All Color Book of Bible Stories*, retold by Patricia J. Hunt (London, UK: Hennerwood, 1978).

3   The only such film I can recommend is the 2003 *The Gospel of John* (The Visual Bible); its screenplay quotes solely from the Good News Bible translation of John.

4   Irenaeus, "Against Heresies," 3:11:7, *Early Christian Fathers*, trans. and ed. Cyril C. Richardson (New York: Macmillan, 1970), 382.

5   See Gordon W. Lathrop, *The Four Gospels on Sunday: The New Testament and the Reform of Christian Worship* (Minneapolis: Fortress, 2012), for a discussion of the reforming intention of these writings.

6   Gottlieb Mittelberger, "Journey to Pennsylvania," in *Pennsylvania Dutch: Folk Spirituality*, ed. Richard W. Wentz (New York: Paulist, 1993), 72.

7   Raymond E. Brown, *The Gospel according to John*, vol. 1 (Garden City, NY: Doubleday, 1966), 3-4.

8   Adrien Nocent, *The Liturgical Year*, trans. Matthew J. O'Connell; introduced, emended, and annotated by Paul Turner; vol. 1: *Advent, Christmas, Epiphany* (Collegeville, MN: Liturgical Press, 2013), 153. For extensive notes on the Luke 2 narrative, see Raymond E. Brown, *The Birth of the Messiah: A Commentary on the Infancy Narratives in Matthew and Luke* (Garden City, NY: Doubleday, 1977), 394-407, 412-27.

9   For extensive notes on the Matthew 2 narrative, see Brown, *The Birth of the Messiah*, 166-200.

Principle 3

ABOUT AN APPROPRIATE
OLD TESTAMENT READING

Just as Moses lifted up the serpent in the wilderness, so must the Son of Man be lifted up, that whoever believes in him may have eternal life. For God so loved the world . . .

John 3:14-16

. . . .

3 Given the fact of biblical intertextuality, the Hebrew scriptures provide necessary context for understanding the Christian scriptures. In the three-year lectionaries, the gospel readings are linked with selections from the Old Testament.

Principle 3 in the lectionary

It is instructive that John 3:16, perhaps the most widely known Bible verse, is immediately preceded by both the obscure title "Son of Man"—an apocalyptic hero of faith rooted in Psalm 8, Daniel 7, and Enoch—and a reference to an odd narrative in Numbers 21 in which the Israelites complained to Moses about the scarcity of food and water. Scholars suggest that the narrative in Numbers is a sanitized memory of Canaanite worship, in which the goddess was depicted as a serpent on a pole: the pole was a reminder of a life-giving tree, and the shedding of the serpent's skin symbolized life continuously renewed. If the Israelites would "look at the serpent of bronze" (Num. 21:9), they would live. In John 3, this memory is set adjacent to the reference to Christ: when believers look with faith on the crucified Son of Man, they will live.[1] The author of the fourth gospel seemed to assume that hearers would recognize this reference to the Pentateuch.

The New Testament is replete with references to the Old Testament. Paul calls Christ "our paschal lamb" (1 Cor. 5:7) and writes of the rock from which the Israelites got water, "the rock was Christ" (1 Cor. 10:4). Paul's letter to the Galatians includes a Christian commentary on Abraham, Sarah, and Hagar. The Gospel according to Mark describes the transfiguration of Christ in a way that is especially meaningful to persons familiar with Moses and Elijah. In Matthew 8:17, that Jesus heals Peter's mother-in-law is said "to fulfill what had been spoken through the prophet Isaiah, 'He took our infirmities and bore our diseases.'" That Jesus told parables is explained as fulfilling the prophet's words, "I will open my mouth to speak in parables" (Matt. 13:35). That Jesus will rise from death after three days is made parallel to the story of Jonah, who was "three days and three nights in the belly of the sea monster" (Matt. 12:40). In the Gospel according to Luke, while on the way to Emmaus, Jesus instructed the disciples in this way: "beginning with Moses and all the prophets, he interpreted to them the things about himself in all the scriptures" (Luke 24:27). A primary key to the intention of John 1:1-5 lies in its parallel with Genesis 1:1-4. The book of Hebrews compares Christ with the Levitical priesthood and his death with the tabernacle sacrifices, and it assumes knowledge of Melchizedek (Heb. 5:6; Gen. 14:18-20).

. . . .

Christians can say very little without borrowing language from the Hebrew scriptures.

. . . .

There is much more: the narrative of the visit of the magi is in part a complex pastiche of Isaiah 60, Psalm 72, and the tale in Numbers 24 about Balaam and the star.[2] Without awareness of this style of biblical rhetoric, believers have searched scientific star charts for a historical verifiability that the storyteller never imagined. One Matthean scholar finds in the narrative of Jesus' entry into Jerusalem reliance on Psalms 8 and 118, Isaiah 56 and 62, Jeremiah 7, and Zechariah 9.[3] According to one Markan scholar, Mark 13:6-31 includes seventeen possible allusions to specific Old Testament passages.[4] Even the four-word summary creed of Christian faith, "Jesus Christ is Lord," is an annotation on the Hebrew scriptures. The name "Jesus" is the Greek form of the Aramaic name *Yeshua*—that is, Joshua—the successor of Moses, who led the Israelites into the promised land. "Christ" is the Greek form of the Hebrew word for messiah, the one anointed by God to reign over the people. One of the meanings of "Lord" is the Christian use of *Adonai,* the Jewish circumlocution for the divine name, as a title for Jesus.

Christians can say very little without borrowing language from the Hebrew scriptures. That in most languages Christians call Easter "Pascha" makes clear that Christ's resurrection is the Christian Passover. Many African American spirituals celebrated this connection between the testaments, their use of the Old Testament becoming a hidden code for both Christian faith and their hope for liberation. In "O Mary, don't you weep, don't you mourn, Pharaoh's army got drownded, O Mary, don't you weep,"[5] Mary Magdalene on Easter Day is made parallel to Moses' sister Miriam—the same name as Mary—dancing in joy after the exodus.

The early church described this phenomenon as "scripture interpreting scripture." Since "the newer covenant" is a commentary on "the older covenant,"[6] knowledge of the older covenant is essential for understanding. Current academic scholarship calls such rhetoric "intertextuality." Biblical scholars agree that "texts do not exist without other texts,"[7] and "each word refers to the many ways in which it has been used before, and opens up new ways in which it can be used in other texts."[8] And not only words: phrases, ideas, and both imaginative and historical narratives are available to the future for reuse. New Testament terms such as the "King of kings," "King of the Jews," "the kingdom of God," "the kingdom of heaven," and the "right hand of the Father" grow out of the root metaphor of Israel's historic monarchy. Repeatedly in the tradition, the prior material is reused in order to support a newer proposition.

The story of Noah's flood exemplifies the church's reliance on biblical intertextuality. Genesis 6:5—9:17 records two interwoven versions of an ancient tale of a flood, described as encompassing the entire earth. Since the rise of scientific verification principles in the West, some Christians have labored to render a single flood narrative from the conflated Genesis accounts and to verify its historicity, thus bolstering its religious reliability. Recent anthropologists have discovered similar flood stories in other ancient cultures. Some scholars maintain that the receding of the ice age led to massive flooding, which may have inspired such stories. Psychologists have suggested that the tale arose from and continues to serve the human unconscious, for each of us has emerged from the waters of the womb. Many Christian children hear an expurgated version of the story that omits any reference to God's destructive wrath. Yet in the children's picture book *Noah's Ark*, author-illustrator Peter Spier adds a startling depiction of the abandoned animals that were left out of the ark, the water rising up their legs.[9] The question remains: What is the best contemporary Christian use of the flood story?

Capitalizing on biblical intertextuality, the New Testament presents Noah's flood as instructive for Christian beliefs. That Christ will inaugurate the eschaton is likened to Noah's attention to the coming catastrophe (Matt. 24:37; Luke 17:26). Believers are to have faith in God, as did Noah (Heb. 11:7), who is lauded as "a herald of righteousness" (2 Pet. 2:5). Especially during the early centuries of the church, the flood story was likened to Christian baptism (1 Pet. 3:18-22). This intertextual usage, depicted on the walls of the catacombs in Rome, heard in the preaching of the church fathers, and echoed in recent liturgical thanksgivings at the font, is found in the three-year lectionaries, both in the Easter Vigil (see chapter 8) and on the first Sunday in Lent in year B. On this Lenten Sunday, the narrative of Jesus' baptism, with God's call to Jesus as he came out of the water and with the Spirit descending like a dove, is set next to Genesis 9:8-17, the conclusion of the Noah story, when God promises a covenant with all creatures of the earth.

Given that the New Testament can be seen as a gloss on the Old, it makes sense for the church to attend to the Old Testament. During those centuries in which the Western lectionary did not include passages from the Old Testament, many sanctuary walls were lavishly painted with illustrations of Old Testament narratives so as to teach these significant connections. One superb example is the Lutheran church in Lohja, Finland, fully painted in the fifteenth century, in which the walls are covered with scenes that chronicle the life of Jesus, with the adjacent areas of the ceiling depicting Old Testament parallels. (The saints are on the pillars.) For example, over the main altar, where worshipers would receive communion, are scenes of the exodus and of manna—which is shaped to resemble communion hosts—raining down to feed the Israelites.

So the question remains: What ought Christians to know about the Bible, given its complicated admixture—sometimes one verse after another—of archaic myth, historical record, religious content, and Christian truth? Choices have been made: for example, the faithful are taught from Genesis 22 that God saved Isaac from his father's knife, but few encounter the story in Judges 11, in which God did not save Jephthah's daughter. In the three-year lectionaries, the key to how Old Testament passages were selected lies in principle 1: the center of every Sunday is Jesus Christ. Thus Old Testament passages in some manner cohere with the gospel's proclamation of New Testament faith. In both the LM and the RCL*, this linkage is present each Sunday, except during the weeks of Easter, when selections from the Acts of the Apostles function as the first reading of the day (see chapter 8).[10] If the primary purpose of the Sunday meeting is the community's nurture in its faith, all biblical selections seek to yield that result. It follows that much of the

Old Testament is not included on Sunday, and Christians of goodwill may disagree about how benign or how problematic these omissions are.

Of the several hundred sets of lectionary readings for Sundays and festival days, the connection between the gospel and the Old Testament is not always as apparent as on the fourth Sunday in Lent in year B, when the gospel reading includes the passage from John 3 with which this chapter opened, and the Old Testament reading in RCL is the narrative from Numbers 21 about the serpent on the pole. Other obvious choices are seen during the summer of year B, when John 6 serves as the gospel reading. During these five weeks, as Christ is proclaimed to be the bread of life, the LM and RCL* tell the Old Testament stories of Elisha feeding the multitude, the Israelites given the manna and quails, Elijah fed by the angel, Wisdom serving a meal of bread and wine, and Joshua leading the Israelites into the promised land. The technique is clear: the intertextuality of the scriptures leads the lectionary to link the gospel selection with the Old Testament passages that enhance our understanding.

In the RCL+, this pattern of complementarity governs the Old Testament selection only from the first Sunday in Advent through Trinity Sunday. For the second, non-festival half of the year, a different manner of dealing with intertextuality is employed. Echoing the ideal in the historic Reformed churches for reading through the entire Bible, chapter by chapter, the RCL+ appoints passages from the Pentateuch during the year of Matthew, given the Matthean interest in Christ as the ultimate Moses; passages from the court histories during the year of Mark, given the Markan focus on Christ as the unexpected, yet anointed, one; and passages from the prophetic writings during the year of Luke, given the Lukan interest in justice for the poor. The hope behind this lectionary decision is that such semicontinuous reading from the Old Testament will expose worshipers to a biblical literacy that is rare in our time. Yet the semicontinuous choices remain Christologically important. Christ as the new Moses, Christ as the hidden Messiah, Christ as the merciful Savior: as with the complementary set, the semicontinuous pattern proclaims the Old Testament as it is pertinent for Christian faith and practice.

The challenge for those who elect the semicontinuous pattern is not only to recognize the sporadic attendance of many church members, but also to retain the fundamental point of the lectionary, namely that Sunday is in the first place the celebration of Jesus Christ. The legends of the patriarchs and matriarchs, the Davidic court adventures, and the struggles of the prophets need to stand next to the cross and empty tomb. If the crucified and risen Christ has been lost behind details of ancient stories, the lectionary has been misconstrued and functions rather as a pedagogical pattern for Bible study. Yet even when teaching biblical content, we ought not merely declaim that Christians should know the Bible. The "why?" must direct any and all biblical study in the church.

. . . .

The technique is clear: the intertextuality of the scriptures leads the lectionary to link the gospel selection with the Old Testament passages that enhance our understanding.

. . . .

Over the centuries Christians have dealt with the Old Testament in three misguided ways that the three-year lectionaries hope to avoid. During the first half of the second century, a theologian named Marcion proposed a solution to the problem of those parts of the Old Testament that distressed him: he advocated that Christians need not read the Old Testament at all. Marcion, who eventually founded his own sectarian community, taught that the God of the Israelites was a deity different from the God revealed in Jesus Christ. In our time, no official Christian group claims such a radical break between the Old and the New Testaments, but some communities might pay so little attention to the Old Testament that the result approximates what Marcion advocated.

A second problematic practice through Christian history is called supersessionism. The idea here is that Christianity has superseded—that is, wholly replaced—Judaism, and so, although consulted as background to Christian faith, the Old Testament is viewed only negatively. One classic liturgical text that expresses such supersessionism is the sermon

"On Pascha" by Melito, a second-century bishop of Sardis. A brilliant rhetorician, he preached the meaning of Christ with multiple parallels from the Old Testament: "Therefore if you wish to see the mystery of the Lord, look at Abel who is similarly murdered, at Isaac who is similarly bound, at Joseph who is similarly sold, at Moses who is similarly exposed, at David who is similarly persecuted. . . ."[11] Yet he used his sermon in large part to blame the Jews for "an unprecedented murder," and with intense hostility he condemned the Jews for the crucifixion: "Bitter for you are the nails you sharpened, bitter for you the false witnesses you instructed . . . bitter for you the thorns you culled, you killed your Lord in the middle of Jerusalem."[12] It is not surprising that centuries of such preaching supported virulent anti-Semitism.

The New Testament's own teaching against supersessionism is found in Romans 11:13-32, in which Paul, having proudly identified himself as a Jew, writes that God continues to nurture the people of Israel. Likening Israel to an olive tree that God has planted, Paul portrays Gentile Christians as a branch newly grafted into the tree. In accord with this metaphor, Christians at their best have recognized in that tree the olive oil that the church can utilize, oil that has anointed Jesus as Messiah and that anoints all Christians in the faith. According to these lectionaries, a Christian use of Israelite stories strives to describe one development of that history, understood through faith in Jesus Christ.

A third mode of thought, less virulent than strict supersessionism but also problematic, has been the development of an elaborate scheme called typology.[13] Here the Old Testament persons, events, and symbols are acknowledged in a positive way, but only because they lead to Christian realities. King David is a type of Christ; the exodus has value only as a type of Christ's resurrection; the paschal lamb is a type of the crucified Christ. One theologian described typology as "the expression of the very design of God."[14] Although even Paul used the language of "type" when contrasting Adam and Christ (Rom. 5:14), the final effect of a thoroughgoing typology can resemble classic supersessionism: the Old Testament finds its value solely as a foil to the New, as if Jewish religious thought and practice were nothing other than a prequel to Christianity. A twentieth-century children's ditty expressed typology in this way: "God had a puzzle plan, of just how things should be. And piece by piece the puzzle grew, like a Purple Puzzle Tree."[15] The "plan" of God sounds like a divine manipulation of devout Jews—a suggestion that many contemporary Christians find an unpalatable way to imagine sacred history.

It is hoped that the three-year lectionaries will avoid these problematic patterns of historic Christian teachings. Contra Marcion, the lectionary family does proclaim the Old Testament. Contra supersessionism, the lectionary values the Jewish tradition as the tree into which the Christian branch has been grafted, the mercy of God revealed in Christ as the same mercy that is attested throughout the Hebrew scriptures to the Jewish people of faith. Contra strict typology, the lectionary does not mean to commandeer the Old Testament for its own purposes, but rather respectfully to borrow vocabulary, imagery, and episode as blessed vehicles for Christian proclamation. It might be helpful for all practitioners of this lectionary family always to imagine that as they interpret Old Testament selections, they are standing next to a devout contemporary Jew, whose current religious practice is also far distant from biblical religion, and who might find the parallels perhaps interesting but never offensive. The oft-repeated image of the two faiths as like an elm tree, in which the trunk is the Hebrew scriptures and the two main branches are post-temple Judaism and Christianity, remains a useful picture for Christians. Our limitless God can maintain mercy for far more than even two branches of the tree of faith.

Principle 3 in wider context

Understanding what our language and culture mean by the words *Jew*, *Judaism*, and *Jewish* is a complex endeavor. Consider, for example, the single word *Jerusalem*, which could refer to an ancient city important to Jews that is now marred by considerable political unrest; a beloved pilgrimage destination for three world religions; a place that, somewhat like Camelot, functioned more in myth than as reality; or a metaphoric name for the Christian church. When contemporary Jews conclude their Passover meal by calling out, "Next year, in Jerusalem," what do they mean?[16] The interpretation of such a phrase depends, of course, on which Jews you ask.

Among religious Jews in the United States, there are at least four different branches of faith and practice. Just as with Christian theology, Jewish law—*halachah*—reflects ongoing interpretation of biblical sources. Orthodox and ultra-Orthodox Jews attempt to live in accordance with the strictest rabbinical legislation, without regard to any historical evolution. Conservative Jews, who treat those traditions as historically conditioned, balance the weight of tradition against the situations of contemporary life. Reform Jews consult the tradition for guidance and insight, but do not claim to live strictly by it. Thus for them an ancient regulation about kosher foods may transfer into a communal diet that reflects moral, ecological sustainability. A small branch of contemporary Jewish practice is the Reconstructionist community, among whom even traditional ways of describing God are rejected as indefensible in our time, while cultural practices of ritual bondedness and communal justice are highly prized. The small number of messianic Jews are more a Judaized form of Christianity than a branch of Judaism. In the twenty-first century, many self-identified Jews are not religiously adherent to any of these groups. For such secular Jews, an annual Passover dinner may be a valued family event, akin to Christmas dinners or Easter egg hunts for countless Americans. The state of Israel understands itself as a Jewish but secular state, in which approximately 20 percent of the population identifies as Orthodox, and where the other branches of what Americans encounter in Judaism are relatively tiny.

• •

Jewish interest in the Hebrew scriptures lies largely in the Pentateuch, while Christian theology has focused far more on the prophets Isaiah and Jeremiah.

• •

Many Jewish people proudly tell the joke that among five rabbis there will be six opinions. It is useful in our time to recognize this wide diversity within Judaism. There ought to be no simplistic notion that all Jews, or even a majority, will share an identical position about religious or secular issues. Any reading of the Hebrew scriptures, whether in a secular classroom or from a Christian lectionary, ought not presume a unified Jewish understanding, historical or contemporary, of such a passage. Even the New Testament refers to several diverse first-century Jewish groups of faith and practice. A criticism of a political stance of the state of Israel ought not be construed as anti-Semitic and, indeed, is frequently offered by Jews themselves.

It is important to remember that all the contemporary branches of Jewish religious practice reflect a radical transformation of biblical religion, which began during the first century CE and intensified after the year 70, when the Roman Empire destroyed the temple in Jerusalem. What had been a sacrificial system under the direction of a priesthood evolved into a home practice maintained by families and, eventually, a public synagogue ritual determined by rabbis. Thus, biblical Judaism is far distant from current Jewish observances. What is taught in some churches, that religious Jews are still awaiting the messiah, is in fact an ill-informed misunderstanding of contemporary Judaism.

Jewish biblical interpretation in both past and present is enhanced by the practice of *midrash*—that is, by supplying imaginative details into the gaps found in the biblical narrative. Such a use of the scriptures as the occasion for storytelling is markedly different from how most Christian theologians have interpreted the Bible. Jewish interest in the Hebrew scriptures lies largely in the Pentateuch, while Christian theology has focused far more on the prophets Isaiah and Jeremiah. Current Christian adaptations of the medieval *seder* for use on Maundy Thursday depend on the mistaken notion that a similar liturgy would have been practiced by Jesus, a proposal that is wholly unsubstantiated by historians. It is important to recognize as well that some Jews judge such a Christian appropriation of their sacred ritual as an offensive sacrilege of their tradition.

Jesus was a Jew, a truth to which the Western world paid little attention for many centuries. What Christians revere as their "Lord's Prayer" shares much with Jewish prayer sources. But historians cannot accurately describe what being a Jew would have meant to a first-century itinerant preacher. Those passages in the New Testament that refer either to Jesus' keeping of the religious tradition or to his criticism of it were written down one to two generations after the life of Jesus and tell us more about the attitudes of the New Testament authors than about Jesus' own religious practice. When asked to describe the first-century synagogue practice of lectionary, a prominent Jewish historian cited the passage in Luke 4 when the scroll is handed to Jesus, concluding, however, that it is unknown whether there was a first-century synagogue lectionary.

Both Jews and Christians borrow from one another's religious past and present. It is hoped that the current reading from the Hebrew scriptures by Christians can contribute positively to a relationship of respect that was sadly missing for many centuries.

Examples of principle 3

Three techniques are repeatedly used in this lectionary family in appointing Old Testament passages: complementarity to the gospel by direct quotation, complementarity by narrative parallel, and complementarity through metaphor. A fourth method, complementarity by contrast, is used in rare cases. The RCL+ in particular utilizes a fifth method, edification by means of biblical history. Let us now attend to the first four techniques.

Fourth Sunday of Advent (RCL, LM), Year A

As the first century progressed, Christians considered which events over Jesus' lifetime manifested the divinity proclaimed by his resurrection. One answer was Jesus' baptism, during which Jesus was named the beloved Son of God. The Lukan narrative of the boy Jesus in the temple testifies that even the adolescent child was the son of the Father. The fourth evangelist goes back furthest, naming the pre-existent Christ as divine from before the creation of the world. According to Matthew, Jesus' conception is testimony to his identity as Son of God. In the three-year lectionaries, Matthew 1:18-25, the story of the annunciation to Joseph of the birth of Jesus, is appointed for the fourth Sunday of Advent in year A.[17]

The Matthean story of Jesus' birth describes a dual identity for Jesus: he was the adoptive son of Joseph, who was himself a son of David and thus in the royal line. Also, Jesus was conceived miraculously, thus revealing his divinity: Jesus is Emmanuel, "God with us." The Old Testament needs to be consulted to understand many details of the Matthean story: the title "messiah," a holy spirit (no capital letters in Greek!), Joseph's dreaming, angelic visitations, the name Jesus, and what is meant by "saving people" and "their sins." Of the various Old Testament passages helpful in explicating Matthew 1, the three-year lectionaries chose a passage from Isaiah that is quoted directly in the evangelist's narrative.

The text of Isaiah 7:10-16 (RCL) or Isaiah 7:10-14 (LM) is situated in about the year 733 BCE, when the prophet, reflecting on the Assyrian conquest of the northern kingdom, Israel, warns the southern kingdom, Judah, to trust in God rather than in political machinations. The Hebrew oracle proclaims that in the length of time in which a young woman can conceive, bear, and begin to raise a son, perhaps a Judean prince, God will deal in some appropriate manner with the kingdom of Judah. Most current biblical interpretation sees this passage not, as did earlier Christian theologians, as Isaiah's miraculous foretelling of the future to be realized in Christ, but rather as yet another episode when God either threatens disaster or offers salvation to the people. By appointing this reading during Advent, the lectionary recalls this sacred history and sets it beside the story of the annunciation.

However, as is usual with the New Testament's citations of the Old, the transfer of Old to New is complex. The Hebrew noun in Isaiah 7:14, *'almah*, "young woman," carries no connotation of virginity. Yet when Jewish scholars translated their scriptures into the Greek of the Septuagint—the translation that was used by first-century Jews far more than was the original Hebrew—the noun *parthenos*, nearly always meaning "virgin woman," was selected. For early Christian theologians endeavoring to acclaim Christ's divinity with reference to his extraordinary birth, the passage in Greek became instrumental in conveying what is usually called "the virgin birth," more accurately termed "the virginal conception." In our time, Mary's virginity is valued as essential doctrine by some Christians, while interpreted as theological metaphor by others. In either case, Matthew 1 attests to the faith that throughout Jesus' entire life, he was God's presence on earth; being the successor of Moses, Jesus is the salvation of the people.

The second reading of the day, Romans 1:1-7, without recourse to the advantages and disadvantages of narrative, proclaims the church's faith: Jesus Christ, son of David and Son of God, is the Lord, revealed in the resurrection "according to the spirit of holiness" as the source of divine grace. Through these readings we face the fact that the Christian faith has evolved over the centuries, through diverse languages, in cultural terms, continuously open to both embellishment and renovation.

Proper 5 (RCL) / Tenth Sunday in Ordinary Time (LM), Year C

Many Old Testament passages are appointed because of narrative parallel. Words or actions ascribed to Jesus are seen as echoing a passage or repeating an action from the Old Testament. The gospel reading of Luke 7:11-17, the story of Jesus raising from death the son of the widow of Nain, attests that even before the resurrection, Jesus spoke the divine word, which had power to bring forth life from death.

Through the principle of complementarity, the lectionary affirms that already in the Old Testament, God's power could hold back and even reverse the finality of death. In the RCL* and the LM, the first reading parallels Luke 7 with a story about Elijah, the prophet second to Moses, as the speaker of God's word and the worker of miracles. In the story from 1 Kings 17:17-24, Elijah invokes God's power to return life to the widow's dead son. The account concludes by asserting that the prophet's ability to engage divine might proves the prophet's authority to preach the word of God. For Christians, Jesus, in some ways embodying Elijah, is indeed the one who speaks the word of God so as to bring life into the world.

By happenstance, the first reading for this Sunday in the RCL+ is 1 Kings 17:8-16, another story of God's miraculous mercy, this time to the starving widow. Because she has welcomed the prophet Elijah, God will ensure that her jar of meal and jug of oil will never empty. It is instructive that in Luke

4:25-26, Jesus compares himself to Elijah, feeding the widow at Zarephath. According to the wider narrative complementarity utilized by the RCL+, the widow ministering to the prophet is seen as parallel to the manner in which the Gospel according to Luke welcomes the outsider, honors women, and focuses on meals.

Proper 6 (RCL) / Eleventh Sunday in Ordinary Time (LM), Year B

A third method used in this lectionary family is complementarity through metaphor. A detail from an Old Testament narrative, poem, or oracle is reused as a figure of speech to illumine Christian belief. In the gospel reading of Mark 4:26-34, the parable of Jesus likens the kingdom of God to the mustard plant, which grows from a tiny seed sown in the ground into branches great enough to provide nests for the birds of the air. For the Christian, the parable points to the resurrection, in which the seed of Jesus' body is planted in the ground, only to rise into new life.

First-century people, however, would have recognized the mustard bush not as a mighty tree but as an annual plant, something like a weed. Biblical intertextuality suggests we look in the Old Testament for interpretive assistance. That "birds of the air can make nests in its shade" is a metaphoric memory of the ancient Near Eastern symbol of the monarch as the nation's tree of life. As described in Ezekiel 17:22-24, the tree under which "every kind of bird will live" is the first reading on this Sunday in the RCL* and the LM. The oracle, in describing a magnificent tree on top of a high mountain, states that God will "bring low the high tree" and "make high the low tree." God will alter expectations about which tree is the best, for God has a hidden way to provide salvation for the people—how very Markan.

Although it is not the intention of RCL+ for the Old Testament readings to parallel the week's gospel, its semicontinuous reading through 1 Samuel brings worshipers to 1 Samuel 15:34—16:13 on the Sunday of the mustard bush. In this narrative, Samuel anoints as Israel's next king none of the seven sons of Jesse who are likely candidates, but rather the youngest son, the shepherd David. Thus just as the mustard bush is described as a mighty tree, so God calls the least one the greatest, and that one receives the Lord's Spirit, as do all believers at baptism.

First Sunday in Lent (RCL, LM), Year A

Only rarely does this lectionary family appoint an Old Testament reading that in some way is opposite to the gospel reading. On the first Sunday in Lent in year A we hear the Matthean version of Jesus' temptation in the wilderness, which contains numerous Old Testament references: the wilderness, Satan, forty days and forty nights, angels, God's providing of bread to the nomads, the expectation that the Messiah would appear in the temple, the memory that God appeared on the top of a mountain. This reading supports a characteristic of Lenten devotion, a focus on resisting temptation. Like Jesus, we are to call upon the word of God for protection and salvation, the word that spoke mercy and forgiveness from the cross.

. . . .

The Old Testament is not the only Christian hermeneutical key, but it does open the first set of doors to the gospels.

. . . .

In year A, the complementary Old Testament passage to the temptation of Jesus is Genesis 2:15-17; 3:1-7 (RCL) or Genesis 2:7-9; 3:1-7 (LM). Popular culture is replete with references to an apple, which appears nowhere in Genesis but arose because of the pun in Latin in which *malus* could mean either "evil" or "apple." While this is linguistically clever, the Genesis story is theologically profound: the tree is the mysterious "tree of knowledge of good and evil" that leads to death. Indeed, humans do search for knowledge, to distinguish good from evil, and at the end, they die. By reversing the values of the ancient Near Eastern myth of the goddess in the tree who, imaged as a serpent, grants knowledge to the woman, the Israelite tale depicts humankind as rejecting the word of God. Both woman and man sin and, in a sentence that has been an endless source of speculation about sexuality, "they knew that they were naked."

According to one unfortunate application of this story, God's curse to the woman in 3:16 led Christian authorities to forbid women from using painkillers during labor: all women were to suffer Eve's punishment. However, the Christian tradition found the primary significance of "the fall" as the explanation of how, after a "very good" creation, God's perfect world became marred by sin and death. Among Christians, "the fall" functioned to teach an essential item of faith, its perpetually engaging details providing the prequel to the crucifixion. The Genesis story pictures the human condition: we are all the first man and the first woman, we all honor what is not honorable, we all eat, we all blame one another, we all die. The second reading on this Sunday, Romans 5:12-19, will keep preachers from blaming women for sin, since Paul, in referring not to Eve, but to Adam, is treating the characters in the Genesis story as symbolic figures. Hope is proclaimed in the gospel reading: Jesus Christ is the Word of God among us, and the baptized share that hope as now they gather around a tree yet more mysterious, the cross of Jesus. Thanks to this Sunday, Lent becomes the communal journey from the primordial garden of Genesis 3 to the Easter garden of John 20.

Such complementarity provided by direct quotation, by parallel narrative, by metaphor, or by contrast trains the Christian community to value the Old Testament as a necessary key when accessing the New. The Old Testament is not the only Christian hermeneutical key, but it does open the first set of doors to the gospels. It has been conjectured that some of the leaders of the church of the late Middle Ages argued against lay access to the scriptures because misinterpretation by poorly educated believers was likely. Answering this concern, it has been one of the central foundational principles of the three-year lectionaries to train Christians in the reading of the Old Testament, no matter how challenging such instruction may be.

NOTES

1   Raymond E. Brown suggests in *The Gospel according to John*, vol. 1, 133, that the evangelist's use of the term *sign*, essential to the fourth gospel, may reiterate the Hebrew and Greek of Numbers 21, in which the word for "pole" can also mean "sign."

2   See Brown, *The Birth of the Messiah*, 166-96.

3   Wilhelmus Johannes Cornelis Weren, *Studies in Matthew's Gospel: Literary Design, Intertextuality, and Social Setting* (Leiden: Brill, 2014), 164.

4   Willem S. Vorster, "Intertextuality and Redaktionsgeschichte," in *Intertextuality in Biblical Writings*, ed. Sipke Draisma (Kampen: Uitgeversmaatschappij J.H. Kok, 1989), 23.

5   African American spiritual, *The United Methodist Hymnal: Book of United Methodist Worship* (Nashville, TN: United Methodist Publishing House, 1989), #134.

6   O'Loughlin, *Making the Most of the Lectionary*, 20.

7   Vorster, "Intertextuality," 7.

8   Weren, *Studies in Matthew's Gospel*, 92.

9   Peter Spier, *Noah's Ark* (New York: Doubleday & Company, 1977), n.p.

10 An adaptation of the RCL gives the option of replacing the Eastertide readings from Acts with selections from the Old Testament, without however reassigning the Acts selections elsewhere in the lectionary. See Episcopal Church, *The Book of Common Prayer* (New York: Seabury, 1977), 894-5, 905-6, 916-17, and Presbyterian Church (U.S.A.), *The Book of Common Worship* (Louisville: Westminster John Knox, 2018), 332-36, 343.

11 *Melito of Sardis: On Pascha and Fragments*, ed. Stuart George Hall (Oxford: Clarendon, 1979), 93.

12 *Melito of Sardis*, 53.

13 A standard text is Leonard Goppelt, *Typos: The Typological Interpretation of the Old Testament in the New*, trans. Donald H. Madvig (Grand Rapids, MI: William B. Eerdmans, 1982).

14 Jean Daniélou, *The Bible and the Liturgy* (Notre Dame: University of Notre Dame Press, 1956), 7.

15 Norman Habel, *The Key to the Purple Puzzle Tree* (St. Louis: Concordia, 1973).

16 Much gratitude to Rabbi Lawrence Hoffman, PhD, for his gracious assistance in editing this discussion of Judaism.

17 This material relies primarily on Brown, *The Birth of the Messiah*, 122-63, 517-31.

Principle 4

ABOUT THE POETIC PSALM RESPONSE

Be filled with the Spirit, as you sing psalms and hymns and spiritual songs among yourselves, singing and making melody to the Lord in your hearts, giving thanks to God the Father at all times and for everything in the name of our Lord Jesus Christ.

Ephesians 5:18-20

4 Since the beginnings of the church, the psalms and other biblical canticles have served Christians as poetic praise and prayer. In the three-year lectionaries, the assembly participates in the proclamation of scripture by singing a psalm or canticle as a metaphorical response to the first reading or to the day as a whole.

Principle 4 in the lectionary

In the New Testament, assemblies of Christian believers are enjoined to continue the communal singing of the traditional Jewish poems that we call "psalms." The Acts of the Apostles models the pattern that was later followed by the church fathers, in which the texts of the psalms function as foundational for Christological doctrine. Over the last two thousand years, monastic communities have steadfastly maintained the discipline of chanting several psalms each day. Reformers such as Martin Luther and hymnwriters such as Isaac Watts versified the psalms into rhyming and rhythmic hymns for accessible congregational use.[1] John Calvin so valued the psalms that he advocated that at public worship Christians ought to sing only the texts of the psalms, never other poetic compositions. In the twentieth century, several denominations renewed their practice of psalm singing—for example, Roman Catholics in reforming daily prayer and Presbyterians in reclaiming congregational psalm singing on the Lord's Day. Both within and outside of public worship, the psalms have functioned to expand believers' imagery for God, the past thus opening windows for the future.

In the twenty-first century, it is largely thanks to the three-year lectionaries that countless Christians have come to adopt these ancient poems into their spirituality. In this lectionary family, each set of readings includes a passage from a psalm or canticle that either responds specifically to the first reading or complements the day or season.[2] Through this sung proclamation of the word of God, whether by all the people, a choir, or a cantor, the whole worshiping assembly is able to benefit from three characteristics of the psalms: they are participatory, metaphoric, and versatile.

First, about participation: Although in some matters churches do well to heed cultural tendencies, in the matter of participatory singing, the church must remain countercultural. In the United States, for example, except for raucous renderings of "Happy Birthday," there is virtually no communal song. Yet Christians sing, thereby experiencing both a heightened endorphin level for each singer and an unforeseen bonding among the individuals. The lectionaries intend that the psalm be sung as communally as possible. The function of the psalm as one way that the entire assembly participates in the proclamation is lost when, as if it is a fourth reading, it is spoken aloud by a single voice. Rather, the psalm in the lectionary resembles the classic Lutheran practice of "the hymn of the day"—that is, a sung text so well-attuned to a specific liturgical day that it becomes not merely a suggested choice but an expected addition to the liturgy. An ecumenical example of this practice is the hymn "All glory, laud, and honor" becoming a designated part of the liturgy on Palm Sunday.[3]

Various musical methods are available for assemblies when singing the psalm response. The text can be that of a biblical translation, its verses chanted from a pointed text, by the full assembly or in dialogue with a choir or cantor; or the assembly can contribute a repeated antiphon to the song of selected singers; or the psalm can be adapted into a metrical hymn that the assembly sings with instrumental accompaniment. No matter how the psalm is musically rendered, the intention ought always to be clear that the psalm is the song of everyone. In singing the psalm, we participate together in the proclaimed word of God.

. . . .

The whole worshiping assembly is able to benefit from three characteristics of the psalms: they are participatory, metaphoric, and versatile.

. . . .

Second, about metaphor: The Bible is marked by several quite different styles of rhetoric. Narrative tells the story of believers, exposition explains belief, and codes describe communal behavior. It is biblical poetry that stretches the boundaries of religious language by providing more imaginative creativity within which the entire assembly can gather when addressing a God who is beyond human speech. The American poet Wallace Stevens defined *metaphor* as the tension produced by talking about two things at the same time.[4] In saying two things simultaneously, metaphor requires time to be received and appreciated. The juxtaposition of the two disparate entities means to surprise the audience, and when the usage becomes so commonplace that the surprise is long gone, we call that a "dead metaphor." In the Bible, it is especially in the book of Psalms that poetic metaphors are found.

The metaphor of God as father, which for many Christians has been so literalized that "father" has morphed into God's name and no longer startles the believer, occurs in the book of Psalms only three times. Rather, the psalms overflow with surprising metaphors piled on top of each other. Consider Psalm 18, in which God is strength, rock, fortress, deliverer, shield, horn of my salvation, temple-dweller, volcano, sky-flyer, a god covered with darkness yet shining with brightness, thunder, support, law-maker, light, warrior, commander of armies—a god who is our stronghold and yet also helps us leap over a wall. The hope for Christian communal singing of the psalter is that its metaphors surprise us with divine grace appropriate to our needs. The metaphors widen our path of faith, offering more space for the whole assembly to journey together. For example, the psalms talk about human fears by imagining a pack of wild dogs, rather than by listing literal personal or communal threats: Haven't we all at some time felt attacked by dogs? The psalm's metaphor can gather us together, the whole Christian community envisioning that pack of dogs also at the foot of the cross.

· ·

For effective use of the psalms, the three-year lectionaries call upon the churches to instruct worshipers as to the Christian meaning of the biblical metaphors.

· ·

Now to versatility: The psalms, participatory and poetic, are applicable to many liturgical times and communal emotions. Wrenching lament in one psalm, exuberant praise in the next, personal struggles in one, tribal memories in another: the psalms are varied enough that the lectionaries can appropriately assign one to each Sunday and festival. Much contemporary poetry is termed "confessional" in that the poet has confessed personal experiences in metaphoric terms, to which the reader listens. The psalms are quite different, in that although some may indeed have been composed by an individual "I," by the time the 150 poems were collated into the prayer book of the Jews, the "I" had come to mean "we." These metaphors bind individuals into one, and at worship—whatever my personal situation, my emotion for the week—we join together with metaphors appropriate to the readings or the season. I may be close to despair, but the psalm may call me to praise. I may be rejoicing over good fortune, but the psalm may invite me to join with those suffering great loss. We are assisted in crossing the great divide between the self and the other by the wonder of metaphor. Joining in the psalms week after week, the assembly cultivates a liturgical spirituality— the baptized community becoming bonded by the lectionary.

For effective use of the psalms, the three-year lectionaries call upon the churches to instruct worshipers as to the Christian meaning of the biblical metaphors. Even in the beloved Psalm 23 are some surprising Christian interpretations. Perhaps the psalm was originally crafted by a poet living in a herding culture. But by the time of Jesus, many urban Jews were far distant from shepherds: the ancient memory remained alive as religious metaphor. In the New Testament, the metaphor has been given Christian interpretation by likening Jesus to a shepherd. By the fourth century, the church fathers, adept in metaphoric speech, taught not only that Jesus is the shepherd, but also that catechesis is the green pastures, baptism the still waters, the gift of the Spirit the restoration, chrismation the oil, the eucharist the table, the Christian life the pathway,[5] and the house of the Lord is both the believers in assembly and the saved in the life to come. Such play with the metaphors of the psalms needs to be taught and cultivated, especially in a society in which many elementary schools stress math rather than poetry.

The diversity of content in the psalms governed their selection for the lectionary. The metaphors in many psalms rely on tribal memories, whether of a shepherding economy or of the cultivation of vineyards or of the reign of a benevolent king or of the protection afforded by life in the city. Other psalms are filled with nature imagery: the rock, the light, the weather, animals, and plants function as metaphors for the things of God. Individual emotion may be likened to contented children playing around the dinner table or to miserable captives being led off to exile. One metaphor that, sad to say, has been lost is that of the Hebrew alphabet itself. Acrostic psalms use the alphabet as the organizing principle of the poem so that the letters themselves become a metaphor for all knowledge, but English translations have found no way to reproduce this technique.

The RCL prefers to include longer excerpts of the psalm, sometimes the entire psalm, which the assembly can sing off the page of a psalm translation. The LM prefers to select from the full psalm those several verses that are most appropriate to the specific occasion.

Principle 4 in wider context

Ours is a culture captivated by fact, digitized by technology. Admittedly, recently the populace has come to realize that what was purported to be fact is, in fact, not fact. But often we wish that it were. We realize that even photographs can be digitally altered and so cannot be taken as factual proof of anything. But fact is desirable, understood to be truth, without which any integrity in democratic government and individual choice is threatened. However, what purports to be a factual account may well be only a mythical memory of the past. Yet many people, insecure in a troubled world, search for refuge in a partial and mostly imaginary view of the past that is masquerading as fact.

This preference for fact enters also the realm of religion: Did the exodus actually occur? Did Jesus really multiply the loaves? Ought an Islamic mosque be built on a location where the Hindu deity Ram was born? People raised in a religious community may reject further participation when they discover that much of what they heard as children is not fact. Meanwhile, others may align themselves with a religious community that promises to deliver only stories that can be literally accepted as fact, as if literalism provides the only available security and truth.

However, no person lives profoundly without metaphor, and human cultures can be in great part understood through an examination of their metaphors.[6] During the twentieth century, linguistic philosophers considered what it is that makes human communication unique to our species, and the answer was metaphor.[7] Humans are perpetually sharing with each other pictures that liken one thing to another, visions of what is not there, words that acquire new connotations. Our body of knowledge accumulates and our community is bonded by means of this habit of likening one thing to another. Thirty thousand years ago humans covered the walls of underground caves with spectacular images of animals—animals that were absent but, by means of the painting, become powerfully present. What is not present, such as a herd of deer, can by means of metaphor bond together the members of the community. Whether comparing a lover to a rose or describing a cosmic phenomenon as a black hole, meaning is transferred from one of us to another by metaphoric language that replaces factual data or fills a knowledge gap with creative imagination. With metaphor, the unknown is likened to the known, and those who share in that transfer—those "in the know"—become in some way a community. The fewer contemporaneous metaphors that persons know, the weaker are the connections that hold them to that society.

In our time, it is largely through the film industry that many contemporary people experience the personal and communal values of metaphor. Are you a Star Trek person or a Star Wars person? Given the multiple hidden meanings conveyed in such complex metaphors, one cannot with much comprehension view first the fourth movie in these series without any knowledge of the first three. Literature functions in the same way, relying on the readers' knowledge of prior fiction for understanding, with no need to check explanatory footnotes. As one secular example, William Faulkner's masterpiece *Absalom, Absalom!* assumes that the readers know 2 Samuel 18—isn't that remarkable? Anyone who imagines that the symbolic worlds of art and religion are readily accessible to the novice underestimates the complexity of the spaghetti strands of metaphors that pile onto the plates that are served up for our communal imaginations.

Although the society relies on facts, culture builds on metaphors. Facts may be processed quickly, while metaphors take time. Facts purport to be straightforward, as if A = a; metaphors present a fascinating journey for human consciousness: A = b and c and perhaps d. We use a factual map to get us to the art museum, and there we experience metaphors that cannot be mapped.

Examples of principle 4

First Sunday of Advent (RCL, LM), Year A

Let us begin at the beginning: the psalm response for the first Sunday of Advent in year A. Another year of grace has begun. The gospel reading is from Matthew 24, in which Jesus describes the coming of the Son of Man. The church has seen in these words the Christian hope for the arrival of God, not only at Christmas and at the end of time, but also now today, in word and sacrament. The first reading is Isaiah 2:1-5, in which the faithful are invited to walk together to "the mountain of the LORD's house" and there to await the coming of God, who promises to bring peace and justice to the earth.

The psalm response is all or some of Psalm 122. In Israelite use, this psalm was meant to be sung during the annual pilgrimage to Jerusalem, when the tribes convened at the central locus of their religious life. As Christians open their new year singing Psalm 122, they join with centuries of Jews marking another year of their communal life. "Jerusalem" is here not only the ancient Israelite city that housed an ancient temple. When Christians sing this psalm, "Jerusalem" and "the house of the LORD" function as metaphors, for it is to this assembly that we are called, where we enter the "city," praising "the name of the LORD." Not only might this psalm remind us to pray for the peace of the current city of Jerusalem, so filled as it is with sorrows and dissension, but to see in the metaphor of the city the churches themselves, ours and all those countless "tribes" throughout the world longing for God's blessings. Verse 2 speaks of the city's gates, which in biblical times functioned as a location of the settling of legal disputes. It was as if, to enter the city, controversies must first be resolved. Christians can see these gates as a metaphor for their entry into the church, quarrels left behind, peace now reigning among the people. Verse 9 speaks of "the house of the LORD our God": that house, for Christians, is multiform, including the very structure in which worship is conducted, this assembly that will soon share together in a meal at the Lord's table, the millions of such houses in which all the baptized gather on Sundays throughout the earth, as well as the house that is called "heaven"—the final gathering of God's peace and justice at the end of time.

With such an understanding of the metaphors in Psalm 122, the assembly is ready to hear the second reading, from Romans, which calls the faithful to awaken from night into Christ's new day. We are to "put on the Lord Jesus Christ"—that is, to don our baptismal garb and live in the light of the resurrection. Thus in this lectionary family, Psalm 122 is not about obscure ancient history: rather, it offers metaphors for the Christian assembly as it enters a new year of God's justice and a share in God's shalom.

Ascension of the Lord (RCL, LM), Years A, B, C

In 1 Samuel 8, the prophet Samuel, by listing all the dangers inherent in kingship, urges the Israelites to resist establishing a monarchy similar to that of their Canaanite neighbors. Yet the people do get their monarchy, for good and for ill, and many psalms are marked by the metaphor of kingship. God is the ultimate sovereign, and because of a cultural trust in the divine right of kings, a quite earthly monarch is granted authority by the divine sovereign, who rules all things from a throne positioned high above the earth. Characteristic of beliefs in the ancient Near East, the current king is lauded as a son of the king, who is the god. These royal psalms convey a worldview that is far distant from that of many twenty-first-century worshipers, for whom the elected head of state receives authority from the electorate, not from a deity reigning from above the sky. Yet granting the timeless power of metaphor, the imagery of beneficent monarchy is alive and well in contemporary speech and the hope for social justice and stability so prevalent that worshipers still find contemporary use for these ancient psalms.

One of the psalms that praises kingship, 47, is appointed in both RCL and LM for Ascension Day.[8] The church, in adopting the chronology told only by the evangelist Luke, keeps the festival of Christ's ascension on the fortieth day of Easter. The first biblical reading for the liturgy is the initial narrative in Acts 1 that describes the aftermath of the ascension, "the day when he was taken up to heaven." Psalm 47, a most appropriate response to the ascension story, calls for the people to clap their hands and to shout and sing loudly for joy, because God, no longer merely like a petty tribal chieftain, is instead "a great king over all the earth." This sovereign God has subdued the people's enemies—and Christians will think of Christ conquering evil—and owns all the shields of the earth—and Christians will trust in Christ's authority over the "cosmic powers of this present darkness" (Eph. 6:12). In our imagination, we hear the trumpet blasts. According to verse 5, God has "gone up" with a shout—whether in a festive procession up to a dais or in the people's faith up above the sky.

The lectionary doubles the metaphor. According to the original Hebrew psalm, God is likened to a king. Without suggesting that the psalmist was mysteriously envisioning Christ, Christians apply this poem to Christ who is God who is the king. Jesus of Nazareth is the incarnation of YHWH, thus also called "the Most High" God; the one dying on the cross is now reigning from a throne, "highly exalted." Christ has "gone up" from the realm of the dead, through the land of the living, into the resurrection life beyond the heavens. In Acts 1:6, Jesus' disciples ask him when "the kingdom" will be restored to Israel; the text of Psalm 47 responds by affirming that the kingdom is in some ways already here, for Christ is already reigning throughout the earth. Although some Christians have dealt with the ascension as if it denotes Christ's departure, Psalm 47 assists believers in acclaiming that the presence of the risen Christ now inhabits the entire creation, with divine authority surpassing that of all others. The difficulty some contemporary Christians have with the dominance of male imagery for God is substantially alleviated as well when applying the metaphor of the king to Jesus Christ. To apply the title "king" to Jesus demonstrates the use of a metaphor, rather than a fact, and a metaphor is always a visit to a realm other than that of literalism.

As an option to Psalm 47, the RCL suggests Psalm 93. In this psalm, God is king not of the people of Abraham but of the whole world, and God exercises sovereignty especially over the wild waters of the earth. Creation is described as God's taming of the waters, and as Christians sing this psalm, they recall salvation both as God drowning the enemy in the sea and as God blessing the waters of the font. Thus the use of this psalm offers a baptismal focus to the royal imagery of the festival of the Ascension.

Passion Sunday and Good Friday (RCL) / Palm Sunday of the Lord's Passion and Good Friday (LM), Years A, B, C

In the three-year lectionaries, the Sunday of the Passion and Good Friday function as doublets of each other. Each year the gospel reading for Passion Sunday is the several chapters from Matthew, Mark, or Luke that narrate the arrest, trial, and crucifixion of Christ, while for Good Friday the gospel reading for every year is the narration of the crucifixion from John. Thus during each liturgical year the faithful hear two different narratives concerning Christ's death.

For the first readings on these two days, both the RCL and LM appoint passages from the Servant Songs of Isaiah 50 and 52–53. According to the Servant Songs, the ideal believer endures intense suffering despite a life of faithfulness, with the hope that the whole people will somehow benefit from such affliction. Jewish readers of these poems have offered various interpretations of this "servant." However, from the earliest centuries of the church, Christians have seen these poems as metaphorical descriptions of the passion and death of Christ. A consensus of contemporary biblical scholars agrees that none of the evangelists was present at the crucifixion, and even when the earliest gospel account was written, many participants, such as Peter, were no longer alive. It appears most likely that some details in the biblical descriptions of the crucifixion were borrowed from the laments of the Servant Songs, in which the suffering one is subjected to insult and spitting and is "despised and rejected by others."

In response to the Servant Songs and in preparation for the reading of the Passion, the lectionaries appoint Psalms 31 and 22, the metaphors in these lament psalms providing yet more details for Christian imagination of a crucifixion at which they were not present. In Psalm 31, a prayer for deliverance from personal enemies, the suffering one is described as being in distress, "the scorn of all my adversaries" and "like a broken vessel." Yet this suffering one prays, "Let your face shine upon your servant," a line that Christians in particular appreciate, in light of their faith in the resurrection. Psalm 22 provides the source for the Markan plea of Christ on the cross, "My God, my God, why have you forsaken me?" In this psalm, the suffering one is "scorned by others," mocked by them (see Mark 15:31 and parallels), and experiences intense thirst (Mark 15:36 and parallels). "A company of evildoers encircles me," and Christians think of the soldiers. Psalm 22:18 provides one of the clearest examples of a metaphoric prequel for the evangelists: "They divide my clothes among themselves, and for my clothing they cast lots" is quoted nearly word for word in Mark 15:24, Matthew 27:35, and Luke 23:34; in John 19:23-24, the psalm is actually cited. Yet Psalm 22 concludes with the victory of the sufferer, who "in the midst of the congregation" will praise God. Thus for Christians, contemplation on the misery of the crucified Christ always turns toward praise of the risen Christ, whom the faithful encounter "in the midst of the congregation." Indeed, the entire reason that the congregation assembles, even when the liturgy focuses on the crucifixion, is thanks to the resurrection.

Ash Wednesday (RCL, LM), Years A, B, C

That Ash Wednesday remains such a popular Christian ritual day attests to the wholeness people experience when expressing the truth: people do choose to mark their faces with ashes, the sign of mortality and the consequence of sin. In the first reading, Joel 2:1-2, 12-17, God calls the people to repent of their sins in solemn ritual behavior, for God will graciously forgive them and will withdraw the possibility of punishment. The RCL offers the option of Isaiah 58:1-12, in which the prophet condemns the people who, although observing such rituals of confession, still oppress the poor. God calls for renewal of life, so that what is now a ruined city can once again be a watered garden.

With either option, the response is Psalm 51, a poem marked by nearly a dozen metaphors. If sin is like dirt, we ask God to wash us clean. If sin breaks the law, we ask to be justified. Although sin is often imagined as adult infractions, we acknowledge that we were sinners as newborns. If we think of sin as having desecrated our dwelling, we will sanctify ourselves as with a ritual of hyssop. If sin has crushed our bones, we ask that our bodies be healed. Our inner self needs an infusion of God's Spirit. If sin has expelled us from God's presence, we ask to be restored. If we have forgotten the commandments, we ask to learn them once again. Even if we fulfill the appointed ritual sacrifices, offering God the blood of our sacrificed animals, we ask God to accept instead a heart bleeding with brokenness. If our lives are like a destroyed city, we ask to be rebuilt. The Hebrew text of Psalm 51 opens with a rubric that, although not included in our ritual song, ties this poem of confession to King David, who, according to 2 Samuel 11–12, was guilty of abuse of power, adultery, murder, theft, and deception and finally admits, "I have sinned against the LORD" (12:13). Thus is added in our imagination yet another metaphor: we are David; although anointed by God in our baptism, we are guilty of multiple sins, and we confess them and plead for forgiveness.

Given the versatility of the psalms, Ash Wednesday is not the only occasion for which this psalm is appointed. In the variants of this lectionary family, Psalm 51 accompanies those who are receiving God's new covenant of mercy, those who danced around the golden calf, those who hear about the guilty King David, and those who know themselves to be Adam and Eve hiding in the garden. Thus on each of these Sundays, worshipers will recall Ash Wednesday. Those who designed the three-year lectionaries had to choose either to appoint as many psalms as possible or to repeat some psalms as particularly worthy. Psalm 51 is one such repeated psalm, and its multiple metaphors render it worthy of its several purposes.

In Psalm 23, imagery from an ancient herding economy has been seen to illumine Christian catechesis. Psalm 122, a song for the Israelites' annual pilgrimage to Jerusalem, provides metaphors for the Christian assembly's entry into a new year of God's justice and a share in God's shalom. In Psalm 47, an archaic poem praising God as a king enlarges the Christian view of the risen Christ. In Psalm 93, the cosmic waters are heard roaring in our font. In Psalms 31 and 22, agonizing individual laments provide imagery for the Christian attention to the crucifixion. With Psalm 51, we engage in multiple metaphors as if joining King David in confessing our sin. We can be grateful that the three-year lectionaries have given us such psalms for our communal singing of scripture.

NOTES

1   This genre continues: see for example David Gambrell's "How Happy Are the Saints of God," a versification of Psalm 1 in Presbyterian Church (U.S.A.), *Glory to God* (Louisville: Westminster John Knox Press, 2013), #457.

2   O'Day and Hackett in *Preaching the Revised Common Lectionary: A Guide* unfortunately misconstrue the intention of the lectionary by referring consistently to the psalm as "Lesson 2."

3   See, for example, the Lutheran *Evangelical Lutheran Worship*, 257, and the Presbyterian *Book of Common Worship* (Louisville: Westminster John Knox Press, 2018), 265.

4   Wallace Stevens, *Opus Posthumous*, ed. Samuel French Morse (New York: Knopf, 1966), 221.

5   Daniélou, *The Bible and the Liturgy*, 177-86.

6   Lakoff and Johnson, *Metaphors We Live By*, 3-32.

7   See, for example, Paul Ricoeur, *The Rule of Metaphor: Multi-disciplinary Studies of the Creation of Meaning in Language*, trans. Robert Czerny (Toronto: University of Toronto Press, 1977), 109-14.

8   These comments on the lectionary psalms have been assisted by William P. Brown, *Seeing the Psalms: A Theology of Metaphor* (Louisville: Westminster John Knox, 2002), 29-30, 187-89, and Irene Nowell, *Sing a New Song: The Psalms in the Sunday Lectionary* (Collegeville: Liturgical Press, 1993), 161-63.

Principle 5

ABOUT THE NEW TESTAMENT WRITINGS AND CHRISTIAN LIVING

Greet all the brothers and sisters with a holy kiss. I solemnly command you by the Lord that this letter be read to all of them.

1 Thessalonians 5:26-27

. . . .

5 A living religion speaks out of the past into the present and the future. In the three-year lectionaries, a selection from the New Testament writings typifies the church's focus on the meaning of Christ for contemporary Christian living.

Principle 5 in the lectionary

We do not know which narratives about Jesus were known to and preached by the apostle Paul during his missionary journeys. However, we do have some of the letters he wrote to Christian communities around the Mediterranean ten to twenty years before the composition of the earliest extant gospel. His epistles—Romans, 1 Corinthians, 2 Corinthians, Galatians, Philippians, Philemon, 1 Thessalonians—have been termed "the Gospel according to Paul."[1] Like the four canonical gospels that are "according to" Matthew, Mark, Luke, and John, Paul's writings proclaim the one gospel of salvation through Jesus Christ in the words and style of that one author.

After Paul's execution in the early 60s, other epistles, literary essays, and an apocalypse that are now included in the New Testament were composed by his successors and by other believers. Biblical scholars have now judged some of these writings to be pseudepigraphal: that is, according to a practice in antiquity by which students honored the authority of their teachers, a later author wrote under the name of Paul, Peter, James, or John. It may be that some preachers hope to shield lay worshipers from such scholarship. Yet even popular media attests to the complexity of the formation of the Bible. Our expectation for honesty in preaching ought to include truthfulness about biblical sources, and preachers should avoid attributing these pseudepigraphal writings to Paul or to Jesus' original disciples.[2] Thus, not "Paul" or "Peter," but "the author" wrote such anonymous passages.

The primary message undergirding all these New Testament texts is that the good news of divine mercy in Christ is not merely information about things that happened in the past. Rather, the good news of the gospel is a current event, its proclamation being inspiration for the living body of Christ, the church. The apostolic letters and New Testament essays affirm that the mystery of Christ is not a "then" but a "now," to be experienced in the first place within the worshipful gathering of the community and consequently in the daily practice of that faith. It is these apostolic writings that taught the church to speak of Christ in the present, and because of the living power of the risen Christ, the baptized assembly recognizes these readings as "word of God, word of life."

Many places in the New Testament address specific issues and controversies, as well as named persons, present to the original audience. What of all this is applicable also for us? For example, is the regulation in 1 Timothy 3:2 that a bishop must be "married only once" meant for the twenty-first century? Ought Romans 13:1-7, which asserts that a nation's governing authorities have been instituted by God, be proclaimed as God's word in a democracy? It is illustrative that neither of these passages is included in our family of lectionaries. Which biblical passages ought our lectionaries to recognize as God's word for our life? To some degree, it was the lectionary committees that made these difficult choices. For example, the passage in 1 Corinthians 7:32-35 that speaks preferentially about those who are unmarried is appointed in the LM, indicating an advantage to the celibate life, but not in the RCL.

· ·

It is these apostolic writings that taught the church to speak of Christ in the present, and because of the living power of the risen Christ, the baptized assembly recognizes these readings as "word of God, word of life."

· ·

The three-year lectionaries employ several patterns for the second readings. Some readings are chosen as appropriate for the day. So, for example, the second reading for Epiphany in all three years is from Ephesians 3: on the day on which the church remembers the adoration by the non-Jewish magi, the reading speaks of the mystery now made known also to Gentiles. The second reading for Pentecost is a passage from 1 Corinthians 12, Romans 8, or Galatians 5, all of which focus on the gift of the Holy Spirit. Some second readings attend not to the specific day, but come from books judged as especially appropriate for the season. For example, 1 Peter, 1 John, and Revelation are selected for the weeks of Easter's fifty days because, with three different emphases, these writings address the difficulties believers will experience while living out the resurrection of Christ in a society of nonbelievers.

Throughout the remainder of the three years, the second readings are appointed in semicontinuous fashion from what were judged to be the most significant parts of New Testament books. In year A, 1 Corinthians, Romans, Philippians, and 1 Thessalonians are featured; in year B, more of 1 Corinthians, 2 Corinthians, Ephesians, James, and Hebrews; and in year C, the remainder of 1 Corinthians, Galatians, Colossians, more of Hebrews, Philemon, 1 Timothy, 2 Timothy, and 2 Thessalonians. Sometimes in a fortuitous way this second reading coordinates with the gospel reading, and often not. Yet the reading can always be heard as situating Christ in the contemporary worshiping church. The reading is "on the horizon, in the background,"[3] calling out to us. For example, on Proper 6 / Eleventh Sunday in Ordinary Time in year C, the gospel reading of the woman bathing Jesus' feet with her tears is preceded by the passage from Galatians 2, in which Paul writes of the grace of God justifying even him. This second reading widens our focus away from narrow attention on a sorrowful first-century woman to what has been termed "the full significance of the Christ event for believers and for all humankind,"[4] to Christ alive in Paul and thus to Christ alive in us.

The New Testament writings differ in the balance of their focus, with some, such as Romans, dealing especially with the person of Christ, and others, such as James, primarily concerned with the Christian ethical life. Both emphases are featured in the lectionaries. Many times the selection on one week will focus on doctrine—that is, on articles of faith—and the selection the next week will attend to the implication of that doctrine in the lives of the baptized—that is, on Christian living. For example, the RCL's second reading for Proper 16, year A, is Romans 12:1-8, a moving description of the diversity within the body of Christ; the following Sunday's reading, Romans 12:9-21, lists the ethical injunctions that follow upon our life in Christ. A similar move from the theological to the practical is found in the LM, with Romans 12:1-2 on the twenty-second Sunday in ordinary time, year A, and Romans 13:8-10 on the following Sunday.

It would be helpful if assemblies could devise some method—perhaps the ubiquitous service folder?—of keeping worshipers alert to what is currently being proclaimed in the second reading. Although it may be easier to attend to the narratives about Jesus or to poetic passages from the Old Testament, the preaching of the church ought not disregard the second readings, for they are models of the essential task of the church: the application of the gospel of Jesus Christ to multiple aspects of contemporary Christian living. That is, Christ must matter now.

. . . .

The New Testament writings differ in the balance of their focus, with some, such as Romans, dealing especially with the person of Christ, and others, such as James, primarily concerned with the Christian ethical life.

. . . .

Currently, few issues are as controversial among Christians and as divisive within churches around the globe as are matters of sexuality. Even during biblical times, sexual patterns changed: the nomadic society of the ancient Israelites, for which a large family work force was required, was polygamous; yet when Israel evolved into an urban society, in which housing was fixed and limited, monogamy became the ethical norm. First polygamy, then monogamy: what now? Because of the currency of this tumultuous issue, much of the rest of this chapter will attend especially to those second readings that deal with gender and sexual relations.

At the outset, it is useful to recognize that the biblical translations from Greek to English that are used during worship evidence some decisions about the New Testament's gendered passages. For example, consider the passage from 1 Thessalonians 5 that headed this chapter, in which the King James Version translated the Greek *tous adelphous pantas* as "all the brethren." Currently, the New American Bible, the New Jerusalem Bible, and the New International Version translate this as "all the brothers." Yet since the original audience did include women, ought a contemporary translation render the greeting as "brothers and sisters"? Thus the New

Revised Standard Version renders this as "all the brothers and sisters." The Revised English Bible has "all our fellow-Christians," the Contemporary English Version, "all his followers." Today's English Version has "Greet all the believers with a brotherly kiss," and *The Message*, "Greet all the followers of Jesus there with a holy embrace." Although this verse is not appointed in the three-year lectionaries, this example demonstrates that in some cases the translation committee has judged what the twenty-first-century church should do with first-century gendered texts. Thus by preferring a specific biblical translation, a denomination has already cast a vote about how at least some of the Bible's gendered passages are to be heard.

Some of the churches using the three-year lectionaries are located in traditional societies that maintain, as much as is possible, a separation between the genders in daily life and communal roles. In the nineteenth century many Christian communities taught that God sanctioned such "separate spheres." The story in Genesis 3 is one example of this pattern: all humans are to labor, but the woman is to bear children and obey her husband, while the man is to work to produce food for everyone. The story of "the fall" is appointed for the first Sunday in Lent, year A, but the gender-specific curses in Genesis 3:16-19 are not included. It is likely that many worshipers are not aware of gender-specific biblical passages that are omitted from this lectionary family, for it is not easy to see what is absent. It is useful to note that 1 Timothy 2:9-15, the New Testament passage with the most comprehensive gender bias—by stipulating women's attire and hair styles, silencing them, blaming Eve for sin, and claiming that women will be saved through childbearing—is not included in the three-year lectionaries.

Many of the Christians who use the three-year lectionaries live in societies in which traditional gender roles and sexual ethics are being challenged. The very first chapter of the Bible is an ancient writing that corresponds with a gender-neutral worldview. In the creation poem of Genesis 1, humans—not merely an original named couple—are created in the divine image, which both males and females share. Both males and females are blessed to bear children, tend the earth, and secure food (Gen. 1:27-30). In the three-year lectionaries, Genesis 1 is proclaimed as the first reading at the Vigil of

Easter: it is as if in the resurrection of Jesus Christ, the cosmos is once again made very good and both men and women live in the divine image.

The third section of this chapter will look at additional gender-specific and gender-blind passages in the three-year lectionaries.

Principle 5 in wider context

Some laws of our lands and many cultural patterns, including those governing sexual activity, show their origins in a past that was markedly different from our own. Humans, like other animals, needed and wanted to keep the species alive. So in the past it was commonplace that communities attempted to regulate sexual activity in order that sexual desires be appropriately channeled and children properly reared. Depending on many factors—for example, whether the communal food sources were plentiful or scarce—cultural variations existed as to with whom and when sexual activity was approved and what the consequences of aberrant behavior were. In the twentieth century, birth control was able to separate sexual relations from childbearing, and the understanding of gender expanded. These realities are among the reasons communities altered traditional sexual mores, changed laws, emended family patterns, and challenged religious teachings, and it has been extraordinarily contentious to defend, effect, and maintain these changes.

Even among persons who urge that men and women be equally valued and paid for their contributions to society, fundamental questions remain. One continuing debate is over what is termed "essentialism": whether or to what degree personality tendencies and various behaviors are essential to the nature of each gender. What is gained, or what distorted, by the practice of "separate spheres"? Are females, on the whole, more nurturing than males? One might judge yes, and then urge that girls be prepared for roles as mothers. Another person might judge no, and then urge that all boys be encouraged to play with dolls. One hears the question of whether there would be less warfare among nations, were over half the governmental authorities female: thus, is the moral makeup of women and men the same, or different? Many people with their ear, and perhaps their heart, tuned to traditional cultural mores, but who reside, and perhaps thrive, in contemporary Western societies, are profoundly conflicted by the many issues concerning gender and sexuality continuously being reexamined in the public square.

One way religion is defined is as a set of communally shared symbols and rituals with their consequent ethical beliefs. A religious ritual—for example, a wedding at which the bride is "given away" by her father to her husband— demonstrates an ethical worldview—in this case, at least originally, that the strong males have control over the weak females. In the classic world religions, contemporary ethical choices concerning sexuality are exceedingly complex. Some adherents trust that such traditional teachings accurately convey the divine will, while other members of the same religious community are convinced that the divine will is being updated, in order to address not the past but the present situation. Some religious communities are somewhat protected from contemporary cultural controversies, but for believers living in mainstream society, religious formation is only one of many influences vying for ethical authority. We might, for example, reflect on the sexual messages delivered by movies, and on the power of films to influence the ethics of their viewers.

Human groups with cultural or religious roots in the distant past must decide how much to maintain their historical positions. An example in government is whether or to what degree courts should interpret the United States Constitution as its authors originally intended. To ensure stability in society, what must stay the same, and what must change? For Christians, which parts of scripture should matter to the present and the future? There are no easy answers to this fundamental inquiry, and the small group that has been granted the power over these decisions is always under the scrutiny of the larger population.

• •

Always the second reading reminds us that the gospel speaks now, to this gathered assembly.

• •

Examples of principle 5

Seventh Sunday after Epiphany (RCL) / Seventh Sunday in Ordinary Time (LM), Year A

We can begin by considering a second reading that has nothing to do with sexual matters, but clearly shows the contemporaneous intentions of the author. On the seventh Sunday after Epiphany in year A, the gospel is Matthew 5:38-48, the section from the Sermon on the Mount urging love for one's enemies: "Be perfect, therefore, as your heavenly Father is perfect." The first reading is the section from Leviticus 19 upon which the Matthean passage comments.

Over the prior weeks, the second readings move semicontinuously through 1 Corinthians, and on this Sunday arrive at 3:16-23. In verses 16 and 17, Paul uses the temple as an image of the Christian person and community. Anyone walking the first-century streets of Corinth was surrounded by temples that honored the many pagan gods and goddesses, and the community to which Paul wrote had many contacts with persons who worshiped at these temples. In verses 18-20, Paul contrasts the gospel with the wisdom of the age. Some residents in Corinth would have granted the highest honor to the kind of human wisdom taught by Greek philosophers, and Paul's audience would have heard these verses as arguing specifically against a popular worldview that opposed Christianity. Finally, in verse 22, by citing "Paul or Apollos or Cephas" by name, the text situates the gospel of Christ precisely within the broad community of believers. The task of the preacher is not only to provide explanations, if need be, of such explicit first-century references, but more to translate them for the current hearers. What are the buildings that line our streets, the worldviews that threaten the faith, the various Christian traditions that seem to oppose each other? Always the second reading reminds us that the gospel speaks now, to this gathered assembly.

Second Sunday after Epiphany (RCL) / Second Sunday in Ordinary Time (LM), Year B

The second reading in year B for the second Sunday after Epiphany is from 1 Corinthians 6 and deals with sexual ethics. Paul prohibits fornication and prostitution. Several biblical translations render the sexual sins more or less explicitly, but the author Paul makes clear the reason for sexual continence among Christians: believers have become one body in Christ, their bodies temples of the Holy Spirit. As in the most profound ethical passages in the New Testament, it is believers' incorporation into the risen Christ that determines their ethics. The lectionary's choices attempt to make clear that one's sexuality—indeed, one's entire ethical stance—is not a private matter; rather, all share in the one body of the crucified and risen Christ.

Proper 10 (RCL) / Fifteenth Sunday in Ordinary Time (LM), Year C
Proper 11 (RCL) / Sixteenth Sunday in Ordinary Time (LM), Year C
Proper 12 (RCL) / Seventeenth Sunday in Ordinary Time (LM), Year C
Proper 13 (RCL) / Eighteenth Sunday in Ordinary Time (LM), Year C

A series of second readings from Colossians over four consecutive weeks during July and August in year C exemplifies the fundamental intention of the apostolic writings: to preach the good news about Jesus Christ and to apply its meaning to the ethical life in a certain time and place. The epistle to the Colossians is most likely a pseudepigraphal Pauline letter urging the believers in Colossae to honor the lordship of Jesus Christ, to live accordingly, and to resist a current fascination for visionary experience. The first two weeks of the four semicontinuous selections focus on Christocentric doctrine. Both lectionaries include Colossians 1:15-20, a poetic passage that was perhaps a communal hymn, in which Christ is acclaimed as the supreme head over all the earth and the whole church, having redeemed us through the blood of his cross and embodying the fullness of God now.

Next come two weeks of passages that proclaim gender-blind ethics. Although not appointing precisely the same verses, both the RCL and the LM draw out the ethical implications of the lordship of Christ. Colossians 2:12 speaks of believers being buried with Christ and now risen to new life. Colossians 3 delineates the ethical life of the baptized: set your minds on Christ, not on immoral behaviors, some of which are here listed, whether actions like fornication or practices such as lying. Believers are clothed "with the new self." These passages make no distinction between the ethics of men and of women. All believers are to be clothed with Christ. The four-week series from Colossians that deals with ethics closes with the non-gender-specific assertion that Christ is all in all.

The further passage, Colossians 3:12-17, is appointed in both the RCL and LM for the first Sunday of Christmas in year C, the date that Roman Catholics designate as "the Holy Family of Jesus, Mary, and Joseph." In this passage, God's chosen ones are called to live exemplary lives, clothing themselves with love, forgiving one another, gathering together for worship, always giving thanks. As is customary in the three-year lectionaries, all these directives are gender-blind.

However, the longer form of the reading in LM adds three more verses, 18-21, which include commands that are gender-specific. Colossians 3:18-25 is one of three biblical iterations of first-century household codes, which are elaborations of the following: (1) Wives, obey your husbands; husbands, be good to your wives. (2) Children, obey your parents; fathers, be good to your children. (3) Slaves, obey your masters; masters, treat your slaves well. How much of these first-century moral injunctions ought to be included in the Sunday lectionary? Christians disagree about whether the male dominance undergirding verses 18-19 especially is God's will for our society. Although the RCL omits this gender-specific passage, the LM retains it.[5]

Ephesians 5:22—6:9 is a lengthier application of the household codes to Christians. This passage is not appointed in the RCL, although the LM appoints those verses dealing with husbands and wives as the longer form of the second reading on the twenty-first Sunday in ordinary time, year B. As for the commentary on the household codes in 1 Peter 2:18—3:7, both the RCL and LM omit verse 18 about slavery and the passage from verses 1-7 about wives and husbands. The lectionaries' handling of the household codes makes apparent that contemporary Christians in similar cultural situations do not agree on which apostolic writings are directly applicable in the twenty-first century.

Fifth Sunday of Easter (RCL, LM), Year C

The five semicontinuous selections from the book of Revelation that are appointed for the second through the sixth Sundays of Easter, year C, include a scriptural passage of gender as metaphor. The lectionary family omits from Sunday proclamation all the violent and arguably misogynist details from this final book of the Bible as less than helpful for contemporary Christian living. The selections in the lectionary come from chapters 1, 5, 7, and 21 of Revelation, and in each case the focus is on the praises of the saints around the throne of the risen Christ, begun already now in the church and continuing at the end of time. Christ is risen, not only then, but now and throughout the future. However, on the fifth Sunday of Easter the selection from Revelation 21 includes the metaphor of marriage: the new city is the bride of the Lamb. Even in the twenty-first century, some languages continue to refer to cities or states with feminine pronouns. For some Christians in our time, this identification of the church with the bride demeans baptized women and intensifies a stereotypical link in many world myths between God and masculinity. Other Christians see this ancient imagery as one that captures something of the intimate relationship between God and believers, and they know that on the following Sunday, the picture of the bride is joined to that of the mountain, the city, the temple, cosmic light, and, in the RCL, the book of life, the river of life, and the tree of life, as all those images are invoked to celebrate the church's life with God.

Receiving and embodying the "word of God, word of life" is always a challenge in the church. As culture changes, with what words ought contemporary believers hear the gospel? When might God oppose cultural change and when approve of it? Does God speak salvation to the world only through the church? In some ethical matters relating to gender, many churches, although practicing baptism equally for women and men, have lagged behind society in advocating changes necessary to improve the lives of women. Christians, however, continue to pray that the Spirit inflame the church through the words of scripture, and users of the three-year lectionaries can pray that through the biblical selections the voice of the Spirit, who is alive and well, will inspire our communal beliefs and practices.

NOTES

1   Raymond F. Collins, *Preaching the Epistles* (New York: Paulist, 1996), 9.

2   Collins, *Preaching the Epistles*, 33.

3   William Skudlarek, *The Word in Worship: Preaching in a Liturgical Context* (Nashville: Abingdon, 1981), 41. See 40-44.

4   Bonneau, *The Sunday Lectionary*, 44.

5   For a thoughtful discussion of the LM's use of the household codes, see Collins, *Preaching the Epistles*, 79-85. For a comment about the RCL's omission of the household codes, see O'Day and Hackett, *Preaching the Revised Common Lectionary*, 146.

Principle 6

ABOUT ADVENT AND HUMAN LONGINGS

Restore us, O God; let your face shine, that we may be saved. . . . Restore us, O God of hosts; let your face shine, that we may be saved. . . . Restore us, O Lord God of hosts; let your face shine, that we may be saved.

Psalm 80:3, 7, 19

. . . .

6 Christians observe the season of Advent as preparation for the coming of God in Christ. In the three-year lectionaries, the Advent readings express the many human longings that manifest our ultimate longing for God.

Principle 6 in the lectionary

Over the centuries Christians have joined with Jews to plead for the salvation that God promises. During Advent in the three-year lectionaries, the fervent petition from Psalm 80—"Restore us, O God"—is appointed several times as the psalm response: on the fourth Sunday of Advent in year A (RCL), on the first Sunday of Advent in year B (RCL, LM), and on the fourth Sunday of Advent in year C (RCL, LM). As the psalm builds to its climax, the plea intensifies—"O God . . . O God of hosts . . . O LORD God of hosts"—as the people call with ever more insistence for God to heed their cry for help. This longing, this hope for the end of human sorrows and for the arrival of joyful peace in God, is what Advent is all about.

Advent gathers up centuries of human longings for divine intervention in our world. A time of waiting for the coming of the light of Christ gives a Christian interpretation to the ancient pagan observance of the Northern Hemisphere's winter solstice.[1] A call for moderation in living, for times of silence, and for the practice of fasting keeps alive an early resistance to the wild Saturnalia celebrations common in the Roman Empire and can stand in our century as rejection of a hedonistic consumer culture.[2] In what may be a legacy from Eastern Christians who scheduled baptisms at Epiphany, churches that stipulate purple as the color of the season stress the penitence required by the faithful as they stand before the judgment of Christ.[3] The coming of Christ can also urge us to lives of prophetic activism toward justice throughout the nations.[4] Additionally, when we face the death that will come to us all, and even when contemplating the eventual end of this entire cosmos, we are called in Advent to hope[5] and to joyous expectation of what God will bring into being.[6]

Because Advent has been observed in various ways since the fourth century, in some places lasting not four but six weeks prior to Christmas, the church's memory carries into the contemporary worship diverse expressions of this hope. Some churches choose blue as the best liturgical color to symbolize this hope. Some Advent devotional guides utilize Advent's four weeks or the four candles on the Advent wreath to guide the faithful through our longings toward God.[7] Many contemporary commentators urge that during Advent the churches resist a pretense that the birth of Jesus has not yet occurred: the risen Christ is present throughout these weeks, sustaining the assembly in prayer.

· ·

This longing, this hope for the end of human sorrows and for the arrival of joyful peace in God, is what Advent is all about.

· ·

In explicating the lectionary's readings, some Roman Catholics cite teachings of the Second Vatican Council to stress the two emphases of Advent: the first, a preparation for the celebration of the incarnation, and the second, a preparation for the eschaton.[8] For some interpreters, the word *eschaton* is understood literally as referring to Christ's "second coming," the end of this world, and the creation of a new world, when God will restore the original perfection of nature and establish an earth with justice for all.[9] For other Christians, the historic emphasis on a literal future apocalypse and on Christ's second coming is better replaced with a recognition of the continual presence of God on this earth, celebrated in each Sunday's liturgy, its power granted now to believers toward the transformation of this world through the Spirit of Christ.[10] One classic explication of Advent envisions that there are three "planes" in liturgical worship: the historical plane, the plane of grace, and the eschatological plane. "The past and the future are only symbols or signposts of today's outpouring of grace. The chief function of the liturgy is to bring *us* divine life *now*."[11]

The thirty-six readings appointed in the lectionaries over the four Sundays of the three years of Advent broaden and deepen one's own preferred petitions so as to articulate the whole world's sad situation. For example, on the first Sunday in year A, the first reading yearns for peace in a time of international distress and for light in a time of darkness; the second reading hopes for a spirit of wakefulness and for upright living in a time marked by immorality; the gospel reading calls for a new world to replace the present one, which seems to be beyond repair. On the third Sunday in year A, the first reading describes the sorrows and joys of the human condition as those who are blind gaining sight, the desert newly filled with pools, and the trackless plain paved with a royal highway appropriate for the processions of the monarch; the second reading employs the imagery of the farmer sowing crops in anticipation of sufficient rains and a good harvest; and the gospel contrasts the clothing and housing of those who are immoral and wealthy with the promise that the blind will see and the poor will receive good news. We could proceed in this way through all three readings, all four Sundays, all three years—adding up to many longings.

• •

The lectionaries' readings remind the church of its countercultural set of values and offer the possibility for Christians to address the world's faulty choices and its disregard of the earth God provides.

• •

Thus Advent lengthens the list of petitions that ought to concern the baptized. It is not only personal peace of mind that is sought, but also the light of the sun, peace between nations, a just society, responsible government, righteous leaders, wholesome cities, a fruitful garden, plentiful food, our fortunes restored. Lutherans might recall Martin Luther's explication of the fourth petition of the Lord's Prayer, in which the plea for "daily bread" includes "food, drink, clothing, shoes, house, farm, fields, livestock, money, property, an upright spouse, upright children, upright members of the household, upright and faithful rulers, good government, good weather, peace, health, decency, honor, good friends, faithful neighbors, and the like."[12] We want evil to be banished, impurities to be burned away, broken branches to sprout blooms, helpless flocks to be tended with care. We want an angel to speak loudly and clearly the very voice of God into a society characterized by self-serving tumult.

In the second half of the twentieth century and now in the beginning of the twenty-first, Christians have joined with many others around the globe to fear the end, not in the terms of ancient apocalypticism, but because

of the threat of ecological disaster. We are witnessing rising seas, the loss
of ice sheets, wildfires, bewildering and destructive weather patterns,
and the consequent danger to numerous species. Far from nurturing the
created order, humans have been busy destroying it. Perhaps a sadly altered
earth, causing untold misery to humankind, and especially to its poorest
populations, recalls the story of Noah that Jesus cites in the gospel for
Advent's first Sunday in year A: "They were eating and drinking . . . and
they knew nothing until the flood came and swept them all away" (Matt.
24:38-39). We now listen with new attention to Advent's prophetic oracles
promising a new earth with lush vegetation and contented animals.

Especially on the third Sundays of Advent comes John the Baptist's call for
the faithful to reflect wisely on their desires. In year A, the wild prophet
in the desert is to be preferred over those wearing soft robes residing in
royal palaces (Matt. 11:2-11). In year B, John the Baptist tells us that we
are looking to the wrong persons for the solutions to our needs (John 1:6-8,
19-28). In year C, we are called to be content with one coat, rather than
two, and to eschew financial improprieties (Luke 3:7-18). The second-
century theologian Origen wrote about the preaching of John the Baptist,
interpreting "every crooked way" as ourselves: "Each one of us was once
crooked; if we are no longer so, it is entirely due to the grace of Christ. By
his coming Jesus my Lord has smoothed out your rough places and changed
your disorderly ways into level paths, so that an even, unimpeded road may
be constructed within you, clear enough for God the Father to walk along,
and Christ the Lord may himself set up his dwelling in your hearts."[13] Note:
"in your hearts," not merely in first-century Palestine.

Thus the lectionaries' readings remind the church of its countercultural
set of values and offer the possibility for Christians to address the world's
faulty choices and its disregard of the earth God provides. Yet throughout
Advent, as we listen closely to all the readings, we come to know how similar
we are to all humanity in our longings: "Think of all the time we have
wasted through recent decades listening to preachers lambast the evils of
commercialism, the materialism of gift-giving, and all of the pagan atrocities
of our cultural holidays, when what we hungered for were words of promise,
of Gospel, of the Coming One."[14] We need not spend time condemning our

neighbors for their cravings. In Advent, we do not long for less than does all humankind: in fact, we long for more, since we long also for God—the God whom we already have. But always we long for more.

Christians proclaim all these longings on Sunday. For believers, all these natural human desires are small pieces of the ultimate human longing, which is for God's very self. We seek the blessing of the risen Christ to be upon us, for God's face to show the world grace and mercy, for the divine peace that passes understanding. All our human longings, whether we realize it or not, are small portions of the wholeness that comes when we are one in God.

Principle 6 in wider context

Anthropologists propose various markers that signify what is unique about our species of *Homo sapiens*. What makes humans what they are? Think of our ancestors nearly 800,000 years ago: cold, afraid of wild animals, wishing for more light, desiring the physical strength afforded by eating cooked meat. These longings are met in the human discovery of the taming of fire. Gathered around a hearth, those early humans found warmth, protection, illumination, a shared meal of protein, and the communal existence without which human life loses much of its meaning. Think of our ancestors nearly 125,000 years ago, desiring to be more attractive than the neighbor, and so crafting and donning jewelry. Perhaps with these shells worn on a cord around my neck I will be better off than I was before, and my pair-bonded partner will be pleased. For it seems that humans always want more: what we have is never enough.

"Survival of the adaptable" is one way to summarize the eons of human history, each period of time marked by a yet longer list of longings.[15] We search for the best way to endure the weather patterns. We reason out ways to interact more effectively with our surroundings. We wear a nicer necklace. The most recent excavations of Stonehenge stun us with the complexity of the extraordinary efforts over a thousand years that this site embodies: many communities traveling great distances to collaborate with others, to bury the ashes of the dead correctly, to celebrate the position of the sun, to join in a lavish annual feast. And now and then there emerged a better idea: first a circular ditch, then wooden posts, then the six-foot blue upright stones, then the 25-ton monoliths, with here and there yet more stones erected—and why? What did each construction crew long for? And why was the site abandoned? We do not know. Indeed, we long to know.

Our dominant culture has a longer list of longings than has any other society in human history. Persons with or without a commitment to any religious practice share in these longings, and for many, the longing also to live ethically and wisely brings with it continual decisions about which longings are appropriate, which will actually deliver what is promised. Many persons long for justice, for themselves and for others. And so citizens of a nation vote for the one they hope is a better candidate, and in campaign speeches and debates we hear nearly mythical imaginings of the possibility of a truly wholesome society.

Perhaps the constant deluge of advertisements—and we might reflect on the millennia of humans who never in their lives encountered a commercial—is one of the progenitors of our age of irony: for we learn while still young that the promise is exaggerated, the slogan is a clever lie. What we long for will not be met by that purchase, that achievement, even that person. Our society's renowned marriage vows articulate this wisdom: the lovers promise a shared life "for better, for worse, for richer, for poorer, in sickness and in health," walking together into a future that cannot possibly fulfill all the hopes of the wedding day. No ancient tale narrates this truth better than does that of the man and the woman in that first garden in Genesis 3. As humans, they of course want more: they seek knowledge of good and evil, independent choice, shared adventure. These they do receive, but they receive the awareness of their own naked vulnerability and their own coming death as well. For if perhaps we get what we long for, we learn with Pandora that opening that box releases much that we did not desire. We may come to wonder whether perhaps the entire experience of hoping and dreaming has been a fruitless endeavor.

The end of each calendar year swamps us with a barrage of longings. It is as if, here at an end, we need once again to articulate all the desires of our hearts, to get these aspirations met before the year is out. So we all join in the search for the holiday gifts that will genuinely bring joy. We assemble family and friends to try once more for the bonds of blood and care. Worn out by all these partial successes—which are sometimes abysmal failures—we make once again a New Year's resolution that means to eliminate from our list of longings what is silly and to focus on one or two of genuine value and consequence.

It is no surprise that it is this human habit of thought and behavior that all the world's religions address, each offering some salvation from our obsessive longings. Buddhism, a religion newly captivating for many in our culture, teaches this wisdom: all human longings, even the desire for a god, are illusory. The only hope is an almost superhuman contentment, a placid acceptance of what is, which will allow for a focus on those in greater need. On the other hand, the classic monotheisms testify that, in the end, the only life-giving longing is met in the embrace with the divine. Welcoming the transcendent involves the community in a different level of pursuit, but one which believers attest does deliver what it promises. For Christians, the list of human longings and the completion of our endless desires are what Advent is all about.

Examples of principle 6

First Sunday of Advent (RCL, LM), Year C

Over a third of the appointed readings for Advent include some reference to the coming Day of the Lord. About half of those readings are examples of classic apocalypticism, a genre that seems to take an almost vindictive pleasure in horrific descriptions of coming terrors. According to the worldview of biblical apocalypticism, the current state of the world is so bad, there is so much injustice, and the righteous people have so little power that the social order cannot be repaired. All things must instead be replaced. The centers of evil will not willingly relinquish their position, so the demolition will have to be violent. The scope of the evil is so massive that only God will be able to effect this overthrow. This classic worldview was borrowed and amended by Marxists, who did not trust even a god to bring justice to the world.

On the other hand, about half of the Advent readings describe "that day" with familiar poems from the Old Testament in which the believer delights in the coming new creation. Believers trust that the presence of God will return the earth to an original paradise and will bring justice to all the world. A universal peace will be enjoyed by humans and animals alike.

Advent's first Sunday in year C is one of several Sundays on which both of these—the horrors and the delights—are appointed. The first reading, Jeremiah 33:14-16, promises a fruitful branch to spring forth with justice and righteousness in the land, while the gospel reading, Luke 21:25-36, predicts "signs in the sun, the moon, and the stars," with nations in distress and the seas churning up danger. Of course, the two expressions, the positive and the negative, are inevitable pairings that articulate the same belief: the old must be eliminated before the new can appear. Both the cataclysmic destruction and the beatific garden are extended metaphors for a single event, the coming of God.

For Christians on Sunday, both are existential realities: the church lives both surrounded by evils and oppressed by injustices, and it gives thanks for the presence of the risen Christ whose power brings about the new creation beginning now. For the faithful, what has begun in the present will come fully into being only in the future, and this conviction keeps the baptized assembly from being content with the current state of social and personal repentance and repair. As humans experience the divine, it is always "already" and "not yet."

Second Sunday of Advent (RCL, LM), Year A

The first reading on this Sunday is Isaiah 11, the splendid poem of the new world, indeed a new earth, that the arrival of God will bring. In the language of the poem, the promise of a restored dynasty will be fulfilled; the new monarch will be wise and righteous, an embodiment of the divine Spirit. The king's reign will achieve equal and impartial justice, which will by necessity include the elimination of the wicked. The earth itself will be restored to an unbelievably perfect paradise, with the predator and the prey resting together in peace. Humans will no longer fear wild animals. Children will be safe. Everyone will have access to the archetypal holy mountain. In sum, every past hope will be met "on that day."

In about 742 BCE, in this and other such oracles the prophet Isaiah called the people of Judah to accept the coming end of their nation. But the end would be followed by something new that would be better than past or present. Christians join with the ancient Jews in this lengthy list of human longings: we want just government, care for the poor, the punishment of evildoers, world peace. In our time, Christians have added to the list our hopes for a restored planet, its animals thriving. Poetic descriptions such as Isaiah 11 of a peaceful paradise became important throughout Christian history as ways to imagine the afterlife. Death itself was accepted as an end of multiple sorrows, for arriving on "that day" would be infinite joys shared in a heaven of the presence of God. In Advent, these human longings turn to Christ, whom we see as just such a lively branch, such a breath of God, such a holy mountain, and we pray for the ability to glimpse even now the new heaven and new earth of the ancient poetry.

Third Sunday of Advent (RCL, LM), Year B

The second reading on this Sunday comes from what is likely the earliest extant Christian writing, Paul's letter to the Thessalonians. Written in about 51, the letter is filled with encouragement for the young community of faith. Although many Christians have kept Advent as a time of quiet waiting, marked by contemplation and retreat from the things of the world, Paul's advice is quite other. At worship, an expert reader needs to proclaim these short sentences with deliberation, so that the whole assembly hears Paul's succinct prose, inviting us all into a renewal of the baptismal life. We join the Thessalonians in their joy, for Christ is risen. Together we pray and give thanks. We are active in the faith, testing, adhering to what is good, abstaining from what is evil. We are to live a blameless life until Christ comes.

As we hear 1 Thessalonians 5 on this Sunday, we have already spoken our countless longings through an oracle from Isaiah 61: we hope for the power of the divine Spirit, good news to the oppressed, liberty to the captives, comfort for the mourners, crowds adorned with garlands of flowers, rebuilt cities, no more robbery, the earth a fruitful garden. For Christians, these longings are directed to God, who alone can grant such blessings of peace. For in Paul's concluding remarks, it is not only Jesus, but the full Trinity whom we welcome. The will of God, the coming of our Lord Jesus Christ, and the lively Spirit: this God is faithful and will act.

Fourth Sunday of Advent (RCL), Year C / Third Sunday of Advent (LM), Year B

Luke 1:46-55, the magnificent hymn historically titled "the Magnificat" that Luke puts into Mary's mouth, is appointed in several places by this lectionary family. In the RCL, it is an optional addition to the gospel reading on the fourth Sunday of Advent in year C, or it can take the role of the psalm response on that Sunday. It is appointed as the psalm response also on the third Sunday of Advent both in year A and in year B. In the LM, this song of Mary functions as the responsorial psalm on the third Sunday in year B. Thus the three-year lectionaries intend that at least once, and perhaps three times, Mary's Magnificat becomes ours during Advent.

Following the scriptures themselves, the three-year lectionaries attend to Mary only occasionally. It is not surprising that the Gospel according to Luke, which deals more with women than do the other gospels, narrates the beloved stories about Mary. Vastly different historical pieties accompany those Sundays on which the readings mention Mary: on the several Sundays of the Christmas season that focus on the child Jesus; in year C, when the mother of Jesus attends the wedding at Cana; on two Sundays when the mother and family of Jesus are mentioned; in the Passion according to John proclaimed on Good Friday each year, when the mother of Jesus is with the beloved disciple at the foot of the cross; and on the seventh Sunday of Easter in year A, when Mary is listed as among the disciples in Jerusalem. However, depending on the spirituality of the assembly, Mary might also receive considerable attention during Advent, at least on each of the fourth Sundays: in year A when the angel announces to Joseph that Mary is pregnant; in year B when Gabriel, the archangel who is to proclaim to the earth the arrival of the eschaton, announces the coming birth to Mary; and in year

C when Mary visits her cousin Elizabeth, who likewise is preternaturally pregnant. In our time, this focus on Mary may be supported by the desire to give Christian women their long-suppressed due and by a willingness for the assembly to speak openly about pregnancy, as well as in accord with a valued tradition of honoring the mother of Jesus.

However, the lectionaries have no intention that Advent become an occasion to praise the wonders of pregnancy—that force of nature that has been responsible for the death of untold millions of women. Rather, Mary is obedient to the word of God and so willingly becomes the mother of Jesus, and believers are called to be like Mary, following God's will and bearing God's Word in the world. In year B this Word of God is named Son of the Most High, inheritor of David's throne, king of an everlasting realm, the holy Son of God. The infant is conceived miraculously, since God alone is the source of a saving sovereign. In year C, Elizabeth uses a title that Luke assigns to the risen Christ, when she refers to Mary as the mother of "my Lord." Thus the faithful do well to attend closely to the text of Mary's song, to learn from her what she expects of this birth.

The Magnificat summarizes all the Old Testament's longings for God's salvation. The song roots the destiny of the coming child in God's ancient promises to Abraham, who in the Jewish tradition is the progenitor of the people. Similar to Hannah's song in 1 Samuel 2 and filled with subtle allusions to the prophets and the psalms, Mary's song praises God for the reversal of all things. A servant has been honored; future generations will remember a young peasant woman; the "arm" of the Lord that brought the Israelites through the sea to freedom is again bringing salvation; the social order has been upturned, the powerful deposed, the lowly enthroned, the hungry fed, the rich sent away empty. Despite what many people assume the goal of religion to be, the God of the Magnificat promises not a stable calm for the individual, but the restructuring of society and repair of the earth. If we are those who are powerful and rich, this song ought to make us uncomfortable: What will happen to our own longings when God arrives?

On the fourth Sunday in Advent in year A, the assembly stands with Joseph, as the angel tells him to name the child Jesus—that is, "YHWH saves"—

for he is Emmanuel, "God is with us." We too want God to be with us.
And throughout Advent, we join in Mary's song. We too seek favor for the
disenfranchised, mercy for all, a leveling of humankind, the feeding of those
who are hungry. Throughout the Old Testament, God speaks countless
promises to the people: we join Mary in believing that God will keep those
promises. The song is a profound condensation of human longings, from the
personal to the social, from the past, through the present, into the future.
In medieval art in the West, Mary was generally depicted wearing red, as
a sign that she reigns as queen of heaven: the things of heaven have come
down to earth. In the nineteenth century, with queens fading away, artists
came to depict Mary in the gentle blue of an obedient young woman: God
is honoring the lowly. In our time, many Christians sing the "Canticle of the
Turning," Rory Cooney's hymn inspired by the Magnificat, in which at the
time of the winter solstice we join in a robust song praising "the day" when
God "is turning the world around," toward justice and peace.[16] Heaven come
to earth, the poor lifted up, the fire of divine justice burning: all three are
partial descriptions of the coming one.

So what is Advent? In the Northern Hemisphere for millennia it has been
the time to hope for the return of the sun; throughout the earth, it is a new
urgency to save the globe itself from human excesses; for Christians, it is
a time to contemplate the transformative power of the incarnation; in our
cities, it is shopping days until Christmas; in our hearts, it is spoken and
untold longings for what is better, what is more, what brings meaning to life.
During Advent in this lectionary family, all three readings for all four weeks
over all three years give to the faithful poetry about the end of evil and the
establishment of paradise; calls to live now, renewed in the presence of God;
the remembrance of those who welcomed the arrival of Christ; and the
support of fellow believers in seeing our longings as met only in God.

NOTES

1 Gordon W. Lathrop, *Proclamation 4, Advent/Christmas*, series B (Minneapolis: Fortress, 1990), 7-10.

2 Maria Boulding, *The Coming of God*, 3rd ed. (Conception, MO: Printery House, 2000), 67-85.

3 O'Day and Hackett, *Preaching the Revised Common Lectionary*, 76.

4 Dorothy Day, *Reflections during Advent: On Prayer, Poverty, Chastity, and Obedience* (Notre Dame, IN: Ave Maria, 1966).

5 John Polkinghorne, *Living with Hope: A Scientist Looks at Advent, Christmas, and Epiphany* (Louisville: Westminster John Knox, 2003), 2-8.

6 Gerald O'Collins, *All Things New: The Promise of Advent, Christmas and the New Year* (New York: Paulist, 1998), 3-40.

7 For example, Melford "Bud" Holland, *Advent Presence: Kissed by the Past, Beckoned by the Future* (New York: Morehouse, 2015); Walter Brueggemann, *Names for the Messiah: An Advent Study* (Louisville: Westminster John Knox, 2016); and Paula Gooder, *The Meaning Is in the Waiting: The Spirit of Advent* (Brewster, MA: Paraclete, 2009).

8 See Bonneau, *The Sunday Lectionary*, 129-40.

9 Nocent, *The Liturgical Year*, vol. 1: *Advent, Christmas, Epiphany*, 54-58.

10 William H. Petersen, *What Are We Waiting For? Re-Imaging Advent for Time to Come* (New York: Church Publishing House, 2017), 10-28.

11 Pius Parsch, *The Church's Year of Grace*, trans. William G. Heidt, vol. 1, *Advent to Candlemas* (Collegeville, MN: Liturgical Press, 1959), 7-12.

12 See "Small Catechism of Martin Luther," in *Evangelical Lutheran Worship*, 1164.

13 Stephen Mark Holmes, ed., *The Fathers on the Sunday Gospels* (Collegeville, MN: Liturgical Press, 2012), 10.

14 J. Neil Alexander, *Waiting for the Coming: The Liturgical Meaning of Advent, Christmas, Epiphany* (Washington, DC: Pastoral Press, 1993), 26-27.

15 Richard Potts and Christopher Sloan, *What Does It Mean to Be Human?* (Washington, DC: National Geographic, 2010). See chapter 3, "Survival of the Adaptable," 44-53.

16 "My Soul Cries Out with a Joyful Shout," *Glory to God*, #100; *Lift Up Your Hearts* (Grand Rapids, MI: Faith Alive Christian Resources, 2013), #69; *Gather*, 3rd ed. (Chicago: GIA Publications, 2011), #622; "Canticle of the Turning," *Evangelical Lutheran Worship*, #723; and others.

Principle 7

ABOUT LENT AND BAPTISMAL IDENTITY

If you offer your food to the hungry
and satisfy the needs of the afflicted, . . .
the LORD will . . . satisfy your needs in parched places. . . .
You shall be like a watered garden,
like a spring of water,
whose waters never fail.

Isaiah 58:10-11

. . . .

7 Many Christians prepare for the annual observances of Holy Week and Easter by keeping the season of Lent. In the three-year lectionaries, Lent focuses on baptismal identity and the consequent amendment of life.

Principle 7 in the lectionary

Lent developed in the third century as a time of preparation for those adults who would be baptized at the Easter festival.[1] Catechumens were invited to intense study of the scriptures, urged to abandon the values of the culture, and called to amendment of life. They would be welcomed into the body of believers after baptism.

However, beginning in the fourth century, Christianity was legalized and became increasingly popular, and infant baptism was regularized. The church, ever creative about its rituals, slowly adapted to the new cultural situation by redirecting the Lenten focus away from an adult catechumenate and toward the vast majority of people who had been baptized as newborns. What developed was a Lenten season marked by penance for those who were accused of serious sin and, for all Christians, by the Lenten disciplines of fasting, giving of alms, and praying, which are proclaimed in the gospel reading on Ash Wednesday. Only after experiencing the rituals of Lent would members of the church be welcomed to the Easter communion. Thus during the medieval Lent, Christians were construed as catechumens once again, since what had been the church's preparation for baptism became an individual's annual rituals of confession and penitence. In recent centuries, many churches also recommended intense meditation on the passion of Christ as an appropriate penitential preparation for Holy Week.

· ·

This lectionary family presents Lent as the time in which to celebrate and explore the meanings of this baptismal identity, as well as to prepare for adult baptisms at the Vigil of Easter.

· ·

In the Western world, this medieval understanding of Lent was supported not so much by the readings in the one-year lectionary,[2] but rather through rituals of daily life. Some of these rituals live on in our time. Recalling the practice of fasting from meat, grocery stores now incongruously advertise,

"It's Lent: eat shrimp!" Because the medieval church stressed that individual sins had necessitated Christ's suffering and death, depriving oneself of necessities or luxuries was honored both as an instance of sharing in the sufferings of Christ and as a symbol of attention to God, rather than to the self. Many Christians "gave up" meat, thus joining with the poor who seldom, if ever, ate meat, and such behaviors continue in our time, despite the fact that shrimp is more expensive than chicken.

Those who developed the three-year lectionaries shared the conviction that the future would look more like the third century than like the tenth or the nineteenth. The cultural and legal hegemony of Christianity is over, fewer governments are preferencing Christian practice, paganism is once more practiced, and martyrdoms are in the news. Now in many places one's religion is seen not as a genetic given but as a personal choice; infants may no longer be routinely baptized, even when a parent is Christian, and when requesting baptism for their newborn, parents are expected—in some places required—to participate in a class that studies the meaning of the Christian faith. Adults are once again presenting themselves as candidates for baptism. So although the rite of baptism had in some places degenerated into a perfunctory procedure that was understood as no more than a pleasant occasion for welcoming an infant into a Christian family, baptism is increasingly recognized as the most significant marker of Christian identity in a post-Christian world. This lectionary family presents Lent as the time in which to celebrate and explore the meanings of this baptismal identity, as well as to prepare for adult baptisms at the Vigil of Easter.

The sacrament of baptism acknowledges that one's personal identity is not a solely private acquisition of individual construction. Along with much else in the human person, baptism sets one's personal identity within the past, present, and even future of a communal identity. In baptism, the past is there, in one's participation in the death and resurrection of Christ and in communion with all the faithful departed. The present is there: the "me" who I am is now a member of the body of Christ, and thus I am connected with the whole of the body of Christ, which connects me with all the needy. The future is there, since at my death I enter fully into that body, and at the end of time, I as one of the whole people of God anticipate being raised into the divine presence.

One recent study of the rituals of Christian life speaks of baptism as turning outsiders into insiders, in establishing "a new and distinct identity for God's people."[3] Although most personal identity markers within our society erect boundaries that separate one group from another, the identity of baptism instead "resists and undermines every power of division and hostility around it."[4] The newly initiated insiders know themselves to have been outsiders and realize their connections with all who are still outsiders. The new identity means not to exclude the others, but to connect the baptized with them. This identity marker is paradoxical by expressing itself as its opposite: the identity of the baptized is not protected by a wall but is accessible through open doors.

To mark believers with baptismal waters, the three-year lectionaries have combined the original and the medieval Lents. As in the original Lent, parishes are urged to use the weeks of Lent to prepare adult candidates for their Easter baptism and for their new identity as Christians. As in the medieval Lent, those who are already baptized are to examine their baptismal identity: Are they living out of the Spirit of the living waters of baptism? Six of the second readings over the three years are taken from Romans, in which Paul discusses how the salvation granted to the individual alters one's identity: there is now a new self in union with Christ. The baptized person "understands herself differently, and thus has new responsibilities in relationship to that new self-understanding."[5] Baptism is thus both a cleansing from personal or inherited sinfulness and a radical alteration of one's very identity. The idea of the six-week Lenten exercise is to reimmerse the whole community into the meanings of Christian baptismal identity. Whether from infancy or from adult conversion onward, Lent means to intensify a Christian's identity with Christ, with one another, and with the needy.

The hope is that, moving away from merely enumerating infractions, Christians use Lent to reexamine the meaning and intention of their baptismal identity, and many of the Lenten readings assist the faithful in this annual exercise by proclaiming the power of baptism, accompanying the catechumens and their sponsors, and inviting all believers to be renewed in the promises and obligations of their baptism. Perhaps this examination will be assisted by persons "giving up" something, if what is relinquished genuinely symbolizes their narrower original self that was deepened and widened in baptism. Even for marginally active Christians, as the church encourages engagement in the experience of Lent, the baptized are reminded of their new identity in Christ: the sacraments are not only "symbols of who we are," but "symbols of who we are called to become" in a post-Christian society.[6]

- -

Lent means to intensify a Christian's identity with Christ, with one another, and with the needy.

- -

In all three years, the gospel reading on the first Sunday in Lent is a synoptic account of the temptation of Jesus. In year A, the Matthean account is set next to the story in Genesis of the primordial sin of the man and the woman in the garden. Thus, we and all our human ancestors have sinned, but Jesus did not, and believers are invited to live, as Romans 5 says it, by the grace of God, as members of the body of Christ. Standing in our baptismal identity, we are called to withstand the temptations of the evil one. In year B, the Markan account is set next to the rainbow of promise at the conclusion of Noah's flood, and according to 1 Peter, baptism is likened to that flood of water that washes away evil and generates a new creation. In Lent the baptized can rejoice in the rainbow as a sign of God's mercy. In year C, the Lukan account of Jesus' temptation is set next to a creed from Deuteronomy, and in the reading from Romans 10 we are invited to join in such a creed of dedication of God. This Sunday is an appropriate time to remind the faithful that the Apostles' Creed is our baptismal creed, and that every time we hear or repeat this "I believe," we stand once again at the font, rejoicing in our salvation.

During Lent are several Sundays when the gospel readings in the RCL and the LM differ from each other. On the second Sunday in Lent in each year, the LM appoints the transfiguration of Jesus. The RCL allows for this same placement of the transfiguration, while providing what has become for many the preferred option: transferring the transfiguration to the last Sunday after Epiphany. In its place on Lent's second Sunday, year A appoints the narrative of Jesus' conversation with Nicodemus about being born from above, year B a Markan passion prediction, and year C Jesus likening himself to a nurturing mother hen. On the fifth Sunday in Lent in year C, the RCL appoints the story in John 12 of Mary of Bethany anointing Jesus' feet, while the LM reading is from John 8 of the woman taken in adultery. Some preachers' guides to the lectionary propose a theme for each week that suggests one specific direction that has been distilled from the readings.[7] Given these rare occasions when the gospel readings of the RCL and the LM differ, denominationally focused commentaries are valuable.

An ecumenical way to provide an overview of Lent is to list the most memorable image included in each reading and to encourage interpreters, both clergy and lay in all church traditions, to apply such biblical images to baptismal renewal. A theme intends to be precise, but an image is multivalent. For example, the image of the rainbow on the second Sunday in Lent in year B suggests the beauty of God's forgiveness, utilizes nature to evoke divine mercy, evokes the entire flood story, brings with it the remembrance of baptism, and recalls the biblical description of the church as our ark. Children can see in the six colors of the rainbow the mystery of the light of Christ. The following listing, which cites the primary images proclaimed on the third and fourth Sundays of years B and C, demonstrates the biblical creativity in offering diverse metaphors both for God and for the life of the baptized.

Primary images on third and fourth Sundays in Lent, years B and C

	First reading	Second reading	Gospel reading
Third Sunday, Year B	The ten commandments	The foolish cross	Jesus the temple
Fourth Sunday, Year B	RCL: Serpents in the wilderness LM: The exile and return	Dead made alive	Christ the serpent, the light
Third Sunday, Year C	RCL: Invitation to the feast LM: Call of Moses	Christ the rock	The fig tree
Fourth Sunday, Year C	Entry into Canaan	New creation	The prodigal son

These images can prove useful in proclaiming the God we worship, teaching the meaning of baptism, and describing the life of the baptized. Take, for example, John 12:20-33, the gospel reading for the fifth Sunday in year B. The baptismal candidates, like the Greeks in the narrative, wish to see Jesus, and in the body of Christ believers do indeed see Jesus. The baptized join with Christ in the death of the seed, being lifted up with him on the cross and thus being brought up into the glory of God. This seed, birthing new life, brings about the judgment of the world, the evil one of Jesus' temptation finally driven out. In this one Johannine passage is found the good news of Jesus Christ and its implications for baptismal identity.

Principle 7 in wider context

Perhaps the stencils of the human hand found in the cave paintings of thirty thousand years ago show the beginnings of the now perennial question, "Who am I?" Although the Amish teach their children the meaning of JOY—Jesus first, Others second, Yourself last—for much of Western culture it is the "I" that remains the center of one's life. As families gather around a one-year-old who is seated before a lighted birthday cake, we celebrate the individual, rearing even a toddler with basics of personal identity: your name, age, family, foods. For much of human history, the particulars of personal identity were given at birth and nurtured by the community, and one had little power to effect any substantive changes. It was a literary innovation when in the year 400, Augustine, composing his *Confessions*, explored his personal identity in great detail and defended his choice for monumental change.

One list of contemporary markers of personal identity includes the following categories: race, ethnicity, nationality, culture, gender, sexuality, physical and mental capacity, family of origin, age, relationships, occupation, possessions, religion, personality, and character.[8] A few of these markers are immutable. However, a recent study of personal identity examines just five categories— creed, country, color, class, and culture—and demonstrates that each is a complex construction of past and present realities, the distinctions more imagined than factual.[9] Thus, labels for one's identity, no matter how central they become in daily life, arise out of communal illusion.

Testing one's DNA, searching for one's birth parents, legalizing a new name, adopting a different religion, assuming a foreign diet, selecting another career, moving to a different country, divorcing a spouse, altering one's gender: increasingly, individuals are granted the right and the permission to challenge given aspects of their identity, to reshape their identity, and to adopt their own descriptive categories. The wider society is learning how to accommodate such changes in personal identity, although societal collaboration relies on some level of personal stability. Thus each identity marker can be traced through what was given by birth, with what that identity had been constructed, what was chosen by the individual, and what the person has decided to change.

The complexity of contemporary society and the lure of individual freedom have led many individuals to focus as much as possible on the "I," to resist religious ties with others, and to avoid societal engagements. Data show that although people continue to enjoy bowling, many no longer join bowling leagues.[10] During the dominance of Christianity in the West, the self was described with religious language: the self resided in an immortal soul, which as the location of "the image of God" was that aspect of the person that would at the end experience resurrection.[11] Yet in our time, the self is less often described as having some religious core. Many persons are identifying themselves as religious "nones"; that is, they do not understand themselves in classic religious terms and have dropped any association in religious organizations, preferring instead to develop an individualized spirituality. It is as if managing one's personal identity were an all-consuming project. Perhaps persons judge their "I" to be the only trustworthy protection against increasing threats from the outside. Serious dedication to some communal identity, whether a bowling league, a labor union, a political party, or a religious assembly, is judged more problematic than valuable.

Yet the vast majority of humans participate to some degree in some religious communal identity, and their personal identity is more or less influenced by a religion, whether given, chosen, or nearby. And although regular participation in religious activities is decreasing, the conversion of adults into a religion of choice is increasing. There is no doubt that the initiatory rituals required of an adult convert and an enthusiastic welcome by the group will in the short term radically alter one's time and energy. However, it remains to be seen how profoundly the communal identity of religious participation will affect either a lifelong member or a convert's ongoing individual identity, and to what degree the communal identity will remain central to one's personality and life choices.

Examples of principle 7

The baptismal emphasis of Lent is made clear primarily with the readings of year A. On its third, fourth, and fifth Sundays, the early church's pattern of biblical readings that accompanied the adult catechumens has been revived. Not only those who are preparing for baptism, but in our time all the baptized, listen to the lengthy conversations that the fourth evangelist narrates. Although it is often the case that the readings in the LM are shorter than those in the RCL, both branches of the lectionary encourage the reading of the entirety of these three Johannine readings, and many assemblies have found effective and lively ways to present these engaging narratives.

Third Sunday in Lent (RCL, LM), Year A

On the third Sunday in Lent, year A, the first reading is the story from Exodus 17 in which God grants to the thirsty Israelites water from the rock. In some medieval churches, worshipers saw depictions of this story painted next to that of the water pouring from the side of Christ dying on the cross. Thus in that artistic tradition, the point of this Exodus story was its effectiveness in illustrating the life that is poured out to believers from Christ.

In the three-year lectionaries, however, Exodus 17 is set alongside the narrative in John 4 of the woman at the well who asks Jesus for the gift of living water. Many Eastern Orthodox Christians know of the icon tradition in which the well by which the woman sits is a cross-shaped immersion font, and it is such an association of Sychar's well with a Christian font that the lectionary presents. The catechumens are likened to the woman seeking water, and the baptized see themselves as the woman who testifies to her neighbors about the wondrous Messiah. All are welcomed into the harvest for which they did not labor. The reading from Romans 5 calls to us sinners, who are now reconciled to God, and so we enter the character of the woman at the well, all of us reconciled sinners. The readings illumine the individual identity of the woman, at first searching for both water and a loving life, and finally incorporated into the plural "we" of John 4:42 and the entire reading from Romans.

Fourth Sunday in Lent (RCL, LM), Year A

On the fourth Sunday in Lent, the gospel reading is the narrative in John 9 of Jesus healing the man born blind. The early church, which commonly referred to baptism as enlightenment, used this story to describe the emergence from darkness that baptism provides. As Christ brought sight to the blind man's eyes and, after a nearly comic episode with various characters of the narrative, to the man's whole self, so do baptismal candidates come to be enlightened, and so do the baptized members of the body of Christ live perpetually washed by the clear waters of the pool. That the name of the pool means "Sent" demonstrates the genius of the evangelist, whose detailed and cleverly constructed narratives accompany the church's understanding of the journey toward, into, and out from the font.

The first reading presents the narrative from 1 Samuel of the prophet's anointing of David to be the heir to Israel's throne. The surprise, even shock, of the story relies on our recalling that in the patriarchal society of the time it would have been Jesse's eldest son upon whom holy oil was poured. Yet it is the young boy, the eighth child—early Christians would have enjoyed speculating about the number eight—who receives the Spirit. The lectionary proposes this narrative as another picture of baptism: we too are the youngest, the least likely candidate, upon which the Spirit of God has been poured. The response that follows is Psalm 23, which includes the line "You anoint my head with oil," for we too are David, and we become heirs to the kingdom of God. That many assemblies are instituting or embellishing the baptismal anointing means that, as the title "Christian" implies, all the baptized are now God's "anointed ones." The second reading from Ephesians develops the imagery of light and calls all the baptized to awaken from sleep, rising into their baptismal identity.

Fifth Sunday in Lent (RCL, LM), Year A

On the fifth Sunday in Lent, the first reading sets the prophet Ezekiel in a valley filled with dry bones. In the RCL, the entire vision of Ezekiel 37 is narrated, and although the LM appoints only the conclusion beginning with verse 12, both proclaim this vision as a picture of baptism. We are daily only dry bones, but baptism is the call to rise from our deaths, enlivened by the spirit that God has given. This passage is set next to the Johannine narrative in chapter 11 of Jesus raising Lazarus from death, which reiterates the imagery from the previous week: in contrast with the darkness of our previous selves, in Christ is light. Lazarus being raised is not in John a description of the final resurrection—Lazarus will die again. Although Martha does anticipate resurrection at the end of time, Jesus says in a typically Johannine fashion, "I am the resurrection and the life." The gospel reading appointed for two weeks before Easter situates the assembly as dead in sin, but Christ, who calls individuals by name, raises us to a new life, a new baptismal identity. We are unbound to live newly, freely. In singing Psalm 130, we acknowledge that we are in "the depths," in the underground chaos of darkness, but we hope for the coming of dawn's light. The second reading from Romans 8 announces our baptismal identity as persons alive in the Spirit of God. Our mortal bodies find their vitality through the indwelling of the Spirit.

Despite its being Lent, all these readings are proclaimed on Sunday and, thus, confirm the assembled body of Christ in the faith of Christ's resurrection. We don the garment of repentance daily, empowered by our baptismal identity as the people of God. Our parched selves receive the water of the Spirit, so that we are empowered to "satisfy the needs of the afflicted" (Isa. 58:10). Baptism quenches our thirst, washes away the dark coverings over our eyes, and assembles our bones into a new body, which is reimagined as the body of Christ, the bodies of all the faithful, and the bodies of all the needy. Lent is like a gateway that we journey through, walking together alongside baptismal waters, heading toward the Son.

NOTES

1   One of many more detailed histories of baptism is Bonneau, *The Sunday Lectionary*, 95-107.

2   One place to find a listing of the one-year lectionary is Martin Connell, *Guide to the Revised Lectionary* (Chicago: Liturgy Training Publications, 1998), 14-16.

3   Benjamin J. Dueholm, *Sacred Signposts: Words, Water, and Other Acts of Resistance* (Grand Rapids, MI: William B. Eerdmans, 2018), 40.

4   Dueholm, *Sacred Signposts*, 59.

5   Valérie Nicolet-Anderson, *Constructing the Self: Thinking with Paul and Michel Foucault* (Tübingen, Germany: Mohr Siebeck, 2012), 54-60, 243-45.

6   Lieven Boeve, "Symbols of Who We Are Called to Become: Sacraments in a Post-Secular and Post-Christian Society," *Studia Liturgica* 48 (2018): 154-55.

7   One example is "Charting Lent," O'Day and Hackett, *Preaching the Revised Common Lectionary*, 106-11.

8   Brian S. Rosner, *Known by God: A Biblical Theology of Personal Identity* (Grand Rapids, MI: Zondervan, 2017), 41.

9   Kwame Anthony Appiah, *The Lies That Bind: Rethinking Identity* (New York: Liveright Publishing Corporation, 2018), 8-12.

10 Robert D. Putnam, *Bowling Alone: The Collapse and Revival of American Community* (New York: Simon & Schuster, 2000), 16. See chapter 4, "Religious Participation," 65-79.

11 Raymond Martin and John Barresi, *The Rise and Fall of Soul and Self* (New York: Columbia University Press, 2006), 41-70.

Principle 8

ABOUT PAST AND PRESENT IN HOLY WEEK AND EASTER

It is the passover of the LORD. . . . This day shall be a day of remembrance for you. You shall celebrate it as a festival to the LORD; throughout your generations you shall observe it as a perpetual ordinance.

Exodus 12:11, 14

For our paschal lamb, Christ, has been sacrificed. Therefore, let us celebrate the festival.

1 Corinthians 5:7-8

. . . .

8 Holy Week and Easter have been observed in many ways since their origin in the second century as the Christianized Passover. In the three-year lectionaries, Holy Week and the Easter paschal celebrations bring both the biblical and the liturgical past into the present.

Principle 8 in the lectionary

Although it appears that during the earliest decades of Christianity, every Sunday was kept as the day of resurrection, by the second century some communities were also keeping an annual festival of commemoration of Christ's passion, death, and resurrection. Liturgical historians have provided extensive descriptions and proposals that trace the centuries-long development of Holy Week and Easter; their complex history need not be repeated here.[1]

Currently, Holy Week and Easter offer the faithful denominationally beloved options of traditional devotions and popular rituals, such as stations of the cross, the seven last words, and tenebrae. Into this crowded week come the three-year lectionaries, which appoint eight days of readings from Passion Sunday through Easter. This chapter will discuss how the lectionaries' eighth foundational principle has constituted Holy Week and Easter: the Bible brings into the present the past records of the death and resurrection of Christ, and the lectionaries' choices bring into the present the past liturgical wisdom concerning which passages of the Bible to feature during this preeminent week in the Christian life.

During Holy Week and Easter, the lectionaries' designated readings are situated within complex communal ritual actions. The biblical readings mean to enlarge these ritual actions with specific Christological significance, while the ritual actions mean to imprint the readings on the very bodies of the worshiping assemblies. Religious publishing houses have provided detailed and creative guides to all the services of Holy Week. These valuable resources are characterized by denominationally chosen terminology for these days and instructions about the preferred method of enacting the rituals.[2]

That worshipers' rituals always affect biblical reception is especially evident during Holy Week. For example, although on Good Friday the proclamation of the Passion from John envisions the cross as the sign of divine life for all, even as it is the throne of the reigning Christ, the ritual of worshipers participating in a penitential rite of reverencing the cross will interweave sinners' lament with Christ's victory. Another example is the Vigil of Easter, which may take place as a monastic meditative ritual conducted in a darkened sanctuary at eleven at night, or may be set in a lively celebration at seven in the evening with all the children of the parish acting out the biblical narratives. Is the Easter Vigil a solemn devotion that prepares for the dawn of the resurrection, or is it the assembly's first exuberant eucharist of Easter? The ritual will substantially affect how the scriptures are received by the worshipers. Yet since the lectionaries themselves do not stipulate which rituals are required or preferred, this chapter will focus on only the appointed biblical readings.

Some of the churches that advocate the use of the RCL have added several Old Testament readings to the list for the Vigil of Easter, the most significant being Jonah 1:1—2:1 and Daniel 3:1-29.[3] As the paintings in the catacombs of Rome and the carvings on ancient Christian sarcophagi make clear, the stories of Jonah saved from the sea and of the three children in the fiery furnace were central to the early Christian imagination of what the resurrection was and is.[4] Although in some worshiping assemblies these additional narratives have become prized features of the Vigil, this chapter will attend only to the readings appointed in the RCL and the LM. Furthermore, although both the RCL and the LM appoint the synoptic resurrection narratives for the Vigil of Easter and John 20 for Easter Day, some users of the RCL have switched these readings. In this way, the synoptic gospel of the year is proclaimed on the Sunday of Easter Day, while all three parts of the Triduum rely on the metaphors from John.[5]

By their extensive readings from the gospels, Christians mean to bring the passion, death, and resurrection of Christ into the present. The proclamation of scripture during Christian worship does not intend to transport the hearers back into a distant past, as might an American Thanksgiving celebration that features a 1621 account of the pilgrims' first harvest feast. Rather, blessed by the power of the Spirit, worshipers are invited to carry the reality of the narratives into the present, with the goal that the biblical narratives be actualized in the contemporary community. The Exultet, the great Easter proclamation, sings out, "This is the night"[6]—Christ is risen *this* night, not a night centuries ago; the date of the resurrection that is featured on the paschal candle is not, say, 33, but the current year. The proclamation of the biblical Easter texts means to say that Christ the Lord is risen *today*. This "today" is built upon the past: pagan springtime rituals, Jewish festival, New Testament accounts of Christ, Christian reliance on metaphor, Easter baptisms, medieval pilgrimages, the usefulness of doublets, and recent biblical scholarship. Yes, Easter has a long backstory.

Prehistoric northern tribes honored the spring equinox as the end of deathly winter and the beginning of another year of life. Later centuries of herders solemnized the springtime by offering a lamb to the divine powers as a sign of devotion and a plea for fertility. Still later in history, and in conjunction with a springtime ritual of unleavened bread, the Israelites added their memory of having been rescued from the death of slavery, and so developed the biblical Pesach, in which the death of the lamb typified life for the community. Adding their own layer, Christians remembered the time of Passover as having coincided with Jesus' execution, and so they spoke about Jesus as the Lamb. Some years after the destruction of the temple, Christians came to adapt the Jewish Pesach into an annual commemoration of Christ's death and resurrection. A Jewish family meal became the communal festival, with the baptized assembly functioning as a fictive family.

The designers of the three-year lectionaries reaffirmed that Easter is the Christian Passover and continued the tradition of computing the date of Easter as the first Sunday after the first full moon after the Northern Hemisphere's spring equinox. Given archaic astronomy, and still maintained by most of the Orthodox world, this meant that Pascha was kept on the Sunday after Pesach. Although current calendars have obscured this connection between the Jewish and Christian festivals, most languages, by calling the Christian festival "Pascha," make the parallel clear. The English language is idiosyncratic in calling the Sunday of the resurrection "Easter," a title derived from the name of a northern pagan goddess of dawn (think "east"). After the destruction of the Jerusalem temple in 70 CE, with priestly sacrifices terminated, the Jewish Pesach evolved into a home meal, and in subsequent centuries it was developed into the Jewish seder. Thus those Christians who during Holy Week keep a Christianized seder are modifying a medieval ritual, and they are asked to consider carefully whether this adaptation of the holiest Jewish festival in a misinformed attempt of literalization is appropriate.

Both the references in the New Testament to Christ as the sacrificial lamb and the second-century controversy as to whether Pascha would be scheduled on Pesach or on the following Sunday manifest the early Christian understanding that Easter is the Christian Passover. The gospel readings for Passion Sunday, appointed from the synoptic gospel of the year, each begin the narrative by recounting Jesus' last supper as a Passover celebration, while the Johannine gospel reading for Good Friday makes the very death of Christ coincide with the slaughter of the lambs for the Passover meal. Although scholars debate the historicity of these early Christian memories, the theological point is undisputed: Jesus' death was interpreted as the culmination of previous beliefs in the sacrifice of a lamb for the salvation of the people.

During the late second century, some Christian communities developed a single annual service of worship that spanned three days, lasting from Thursday through Sunday. Called in Latin the *Triduum* and in English the "great Three Days," this ritual holds together theologically the last supper, Jesus' arrest, trial, execution, burial, and resurrection. In this way each episode of the story is part of the whole and takes its specific meaning from the whole. The designers of the three-year lectionaries have adopted this pattern.

The early centuries of the church established a reliance on the technique of metaphor, which, for example, is central to the Johannine passion narrative appointed for Holy Thursday and Good Friday.[7] That John 13 begins the Passion with Jesus washing his disciples' feet explicates metaphorically Christ's call to servanthood. In John 19, when on the cross Jesus is given wine to drink, hyssop is used. Hyssop, a wholly unlikely plant to serve as a sponge, metaphorically connects Jesus with the paschal lamb, which was served with the herb. In the Johannine account, it is not women who are to anoint Jesus' body after the sabbath. Rather, Jesus is buried with a staggering hundred pounds of spices—again, most likely a Johannine metaphor designating Christ's kingly status. Furthermore, Jesus is buried in a garden.

WORD OF GOD, WORD OF LIFE

In the first century, gardens were a privileged use of land for beauty and pleasure, generally associated with monarchs—not, as in Victorian times, places of burial. Yet for the fourth evangelist, the place of Jesus' burial is the site of the new life of the monarch.

This lectionary family adopts another significant feature of second-century communities: Easter as the optimal occasion for baptisms. This historic practice is recalled in Romans 6:3-11, the New Testament reading for the Vigil of Easter, in which baptism is interpreted as the believers' incorporation into the death and resurrection of Christ. It is as if the sacrament of baptism is a supreme metaphor, an enacted sign of a multitude of meanings. That some Christians are once again designating the Easter Vigil as a preferred time for parish baptisms helps to bring into the present the best of historic liturgical practice.

Although the second century featured metaphor, the fourth century highlighted memory. At that time began the phenomenon of pilgrimages to Jerusalem, where local Christians had developed a walkabout that traversed the movements of Jesus during his last week. Egeria's famous memoir recounts the carefully constructed rituals of appropriate Bible readings and prayers that made the memory of the passion come alive for believers.[8] By visiting all the sites of Jesus' passion and death the faithful could repeat the past in the present. The journey seared the biblical narrative into their memories. By the eighth century, various practices of walking the way of the cross became widespread, and in our time, films loosely based on the Bible attempt to present what happened historically, thus inserting into viewers' minds a kind of memory of the events of Jesus' life and death.

Liturgy as memory is seen also in what the three-year lectionaries appoint for the palm procession. As the opening reading on Passion Sunday, a synoptic account of Jesus' entry in Jerusalem is proclaimed, and since many churches accompany the reading with an enacted procession around the church, inside or outside, with everyone waving their palms, the reading helps the faithful to remember the opening of Holy Week. The communal response for the palm procession is Psalm 118:1-2, 19-29. According to this song of praise, the community is walking together through the gates into the city, while lauding the cornerstone of the building they enter. By enacting the memory of ancient Israelites entering the holy city and of first-century Jews lauding the coming Messiah, contemporary worshipers praise Christ, the cornerstone of their city of God, and so situate their own movements into Christian memory.

That the three-year lectionaries appoint the full or a shortened passion account from the synoptic gospels for the Sunday of the Passion also leans on memory. The synoptics feel like memory: each episode is narrated clearly, logically following what went before, and only rarely (for example, the disciple running away naked in Mark 14:52) is there an incongruous detail. It is important, however, that current believers, who naturally assume that such biblical accounts are historically accurate, not be encouraged to imagine that Matthew 26–27, Mark 14–15, and Luke 22–23 are precise accounts of first-century events. None of the evangelists was present during these events, all rely on poetic imagery from the Old Testament to describe Jesus' suffering, and any attentive worshipers will discern differences among the narratives. In the scriptures, memory is shaped by belief: all the evangelists shape the accounts they have received to serve their theological purposes. Yet granting these caveats, the synoptic accounts of the passion proclaimed on Passion Sunday serve to remind believers each year of the history of the suffering and death of Christ.

Christmas has long been celebrated with a doublet: Luke 2 proclaimed on Christmas Eve and John 1 on Christmas Day. When the three-year lectionaries were designed in the twentieth century, this technique of doublets was applied also to Holy Week. On Passion Sunday, the synoptic gospel of the year is read. These narratives share the understanding that the victim Jesus suffered throughout his ordeal and died in great pain. Yet these records of his pain and our lament over it are scheduled on Sunday, which is always the day of the resurrection; thus the lectionary expresses the profound paradox of the faith: death and life interwoven together.

The second of this doublet takes place on Good Friday. In the Johannine account of the passion, there is no kiss of Judas; rather, Jesus goes forward to meet his death. An entire cohort (that's six hundred Roman soldiers!) comes to arrest Jesus, and they fall at his feet when he calls out, *"Ego eimi*; I AM." Jesus debates with Pilate, is arrayed in a purple robe, and from the cross attends to his family and followers. Not a silent victim, this Jesus is the Word of God who at his death "gave up his spirit." Once again proclaiming the paradoxes of the faith, the lectionaries assign this testimony of the reigning Christ to the weekday which is the commemoration of Jesus' execution. As does Passion Sunday, Good Friday attends to both death and life.

Another doublet is assigned to Easter itself. Each year, one synoptic account and John 20 are proclaimed, and in year B Paul's description in 1 Corinthians 15 of Jesus' resurrection appearances is also appointed. Thus both the great Vigil of Easter and Easter Day proclaim the resurrection, Pascha celebrated at night and then differently in the morning. These variations assist the assembly in honoring the mystery of Christ's resurrection, the lectionaries offering testimony to the divine victory over death and to the community's joy in experiencing the ongoing life of Christ in this assembly.

· ·

As does Passion Sunday, Good Friday attends to both death and life.

· ·

Principle 8 in wider context

To mark the relationship between past and present, humans organize their individual and communal experiences with several layers of timekeeping. First, there is the situation of the cosmos: What is communal time in relation to the sun? So, we say, what time is it? How will humans order their lives and ensure their food supply, given the movements of the cosmos? It is not surprising that ancient humans gathered for annual feasts at the times of the solstices and equinoxes. Greeting-card companies are meeting a renewed interest in winter solstice celebrations, and even the current date of Easter is determined by the relationship between the earth and the sun.

A second layer of timekeeping is that of the tribal memory: What were the seminal events in the past that must be commemorated so that the present community stands rightly in relation to its past? The international community remembers an armistice; the nation, the death dates of its founders; and the family, its birthdays and anniversaries. Each of these imprints itself on the present: this is part of who you are. Despite the current American lure of moving to a new place and establishing a new identity, the search for one's ancestors is an increasingly popular hobby these days, as if these ancestors can offer the key to one's identity. For religious communities, there will be many or few anniversaries observed, perhaps only of the founder, or perhaps of dozens of the followers. The idea has been that knowledge of those who lived in the past gives an added dimension to the small private life of each individual. A third calendar—for some people the most significant—is the personal: my birthday and the dates of my achievements. Yet in a thriving community, that personal time is made broader by being celebrated by the many.

Each of these methods of timekeeping helps maintain present communal stability by the joint repetition of past shared values. When blasts from horrific bombs are turned into the delight of fireworks, the sorrowful horror has been recast as current entertainment. We think of all the advice columnists who are asked how a person is to recover from the hurt of a forgotten anniversary or a boycotted celebration. Since communal participation in the various layers of timekeeping glues the community together, an absence in the past sometimes unglued the relationship. There were times and places in European history when a person who had been absent from the Easter celebration was no longer considered to be Christian, for then, as now, the community hoped to pressure individuals to show present reverence for the communal past.

Yet many questions remain: What part of the past ought to be recalled and celebrated in the present? What from the American Civil War ought to be remembered? The statues of which persons should be treasured? What was the European immigration into North America really like? What ought to be recalled with pride and what with shame? Who decides? Ought elementary school children be required to recite a pledge of allegiance? Which stories about the deceased can be told at the meal following a funeral, and which should be interred along with the corpse? The historical record is full of holes, marked by exaggerations, riddled with errors of memory. Much of what was past has been appropriately discarded before the present: we no longer expose newborns who have disabilities, we no longer force our adolescent daughters into arranged marriages, we no longer tout our slaves. Thus while the activity of honoring the past is prized among humans, such celebrations are of necessity part whitewash. Can the community celebrate the past while distancing itself from past values? When at a wedding a father calls out "I do," thus presenting his daughter as bride to her new husband, what is the meaning of these words if the couple has been living together for years? Do past words take on an altered meaning when spoken in the present?

Religions are constantly addressing these questions as they consider how to keep their own tribal calendar. For an example in Christianity: one gospel tells the story of Jesus washing his disciples' feet. Did that actually happen? What would it have meant to its original participants? Should it be narrated as significant for our time? If the story is ritually enacted, ought it be somehow adapted for the present, perhaps changed into the polishing of shoes or the washing of hands? Who gets to decide? How does the narrative of the footwashing function in the consciousness of those persons who attend the service? Will several or many years of repetition of the story be required for any effect to be evident? Will there be any discernable difference between those members of the community who attend to this narrative and those who do not?

Asked most simply, how is the past alive in the present? Indeed, how much ought the past to matter in the present? Each human community must inquire how best to keep its past alive in its present, as well as whether some of its past, and even of its present, is best buried deep underground, nevermore to exert any authority in the future.

Examples of principle 8

Holy Thursday (RCL, LM), Years A, B, C

Named by some churches "Maundy Thursday" for Jesus' *mandatum*, or "command," to love one another, the Thursday of Holy Week exemplifies the lectionaries' intention to bring the past into the present. The first reading from Exodus 12 describes the Israelite Pesach. Its citation of God's command to Moses to prepare the first Passover took its literary form centuries after the exodus, during the Babylonian exile, by which time the annual Pesach combined three different rituals: an ancient nomadic rite in which a yearling lamb was sacrificed and eaten; a later agricultural springtime ritual, in which the sharing of unleavened bread celebrated the barley harvest; and the reenactment of each family's final meal before fleeing slavery in Egypt. With this reading during Holy Week, Christians add themselves to this layered chronology of salvation, the current worshipers seeing the death of Christ as something like the slaughter of those sheep and goats, and the sharing of bread and wine as recalling that ancient meal of deliverance. The ancient Israelites considered that the life of a being resided in its blood, and so their smearing of their doorposts with the lamb's blood signified their prayer to God for protection from death. In a parallel fashion, Christians think of the blood of Christ marking the doors of their hearts. The reading from the book of Exodus concludes with the solemn pronouncement that the Passover with all its historical memories is to be repeated annually, for the salvation of the gathered community. In the communal response from Psalm 116 the contemporary assembly praises God for saving its life. Joining the ancient Jews, we too lift the cup of salvation and offer the sacrifice of thanksgiving.

The second reading quotes Paul, who in 1 Corinthians is instructing the community toward a more appropriate manner in which to hold their communion ritual. Even before the composition of the gospels, Christians were gathering to share bread and wine "in remembrance" of the Lord. The cup of this meal is described as "the new covenant" in Jesus' blood, language which reinterprets the traditional understanding of the covenant between God and the people Israel. The ancient sense that the blood provides life has been retained. Yet Paul chastises the Corinthians for turning this sacred meal into some kind of insiders' party, when instead it means to bond together the entire community into the death of Christ. By hearing this reading on Holy Thursday, the contemporary assembly joins with Jesus in his death, the past words of Christ operative in the present.

By appointing as the gospel reading the Johannine account of Jesus' last supper, the lectionaries present the dictum of the New Testament: that the life and death of Jesus turns us to serve our neighbor. In the Gospel according to John, it was love that from the beginning (see John 1:18— "the Father's heart") characterized divine activity and now impels the community, and Jesus symbolized this love in the menial task of the washing of the feet.

The reading from John 13 invites us to trace the use of the term *body* through the scriptures. On Holy Thursday we first encounter the dead bodies of the lambs and the living bodies of the freed Israelites. Next, we join with the bodies of the Jews keeping a Pesach of thanksgiving. Then we join with Paul in sharing the bread of the meal and the body of the crucified and risen Christ. Finally, in the mystery of the incarnation, we see that the body of Christ is not only the bread in the presider's hands, the person of Christ on the cross, and the piece of bread we consume, but also the very feet of those worshiping with us this evening. On Holy Thursday the lectionaries present a stunning summary of biblical faith: the first and repeated Pesach leading to the last meal of Jesus; the blood on the door, the blood on the cross, and the blood in the cup; the body of Christ, the body of the community, the bodies of our neighbors. It may take many years of attending to these readings to live fully into them. And Thursday is only the beginning of the great Three Days.

Easter Vigil (RCL), Easter Sunday at the Easter Vigil (LM), Years A, B, C

The RCL appoints nine Old Testament readings for the Vigil, and the LM seven. Each of these readings deals with both death and life. Each portrays God in a distinctive way. Each features in the biblical story of salvation. Each informs baptismal catechesis. Thus, like Holy Thursday, the Vigil is shaped by metaphor, memory, and liturgical history and practice.

The first reading for the Vigil is the liturgical poem of creation in Genesis 1. It was common in antiquity that at the annual primary religious festival, the elders repeated the story of the creation of the universe. According to Genesis, the vivifying word of God is spoken into the original chaos. Christians also begin their story of salvation with God's benevolent creation of all that exists. In this story God is the mighty creator, outside the universe, the deity beyond all things, speaking into existence the increasing complexity of life. As God hovers over the waters, Christians see the Spirit of God hovering over the font, bringing forth the life of the baptized. In this story, God brings life where there is no life, just as God does in the resurrection of Christ.

In the RCL, the second suggested reading is the story of Noah's flood. Scholars of myth see this legend as yet another creation story: there are once again the waters of chaos, and God brings forth life. In this beloved tale of God's salvation, divine mercy places the faithful few into a new world redolent with life. In this reading, God is the destroyer of evil, the washerwoman who cleans a dirty world. The ark is the church, or God is the ark, holding us with care, and God is the dove, flying into the new world with peace. In 1 Peter 3:18-22, Christians applied this story to baptism, its waters washing away sin. Noah's flood is also an image of the resurrection, all evil giving way to God's new life.

The next reading (RCL, LM) is the tale in Genesis 22 of the testing of Abraham, also called over the centuries the "sacrifice of Isaac," although Isaac is not sacrificed. Jews and Christians alike have faced this troubling story, seeing in it a God whose word is inexplicable, yet whose final gift is salvation. No longer is the firstborn son to be killed to appease the deity. Now God saves the child, and in baptism we are that child. Christ is the ram, taking our place, going into death for us and rising from the tomb.

Usually understood as the second most important reading of the Vigil, the narrative of the crossing of the sea in Exodus 14–15 comes next (RCL, LM). God is the liberator who wins victory for the oppressed, saving the Israelites from slavery. God is seen in the protective cloud that stands behind the Israelites and the light of fire that goes before them. Early

Christian preachers saw in Moses' staff a depiction of the cross itself. If literalized, this story has a disturbing conclusion, since God destroys the entire Egyptian army, many of its soldiers merely serving their monarch. However, in Christian tradition, the story functions as a metaphor that praises God for saving the people; in the LM, worshipers join with Moses to sing praise, and in the RCL, Miriam invites them to dance on the safe side of the sea. Christians have likened baptism to this sea, through which the faithful are led from death to life. As a resurrection story, the parting of the waters functions like the rending of the tomb; ahead are the gardens of the promised land.

In that these readings transport the worshipers through the history of Israel, in Isaiah 54 (LM) the hearers are now in exile, seemingly abandoned by the divine. Yet in this reading the images of the saving God are proclaimed one after another. Although we are surrounded by death, the prophet proclaims the good news that God is married to us, committed to us in love. God is our redeemer, having bought us back from the enslaving power of evil. God is the peacemaker, the teacher of the youth. In rebuilding the city, God will construct streets of gems, buildings of jewels, city walls that are showcases of precious stones. Baptism is our covenant of peace, and the restored and glistening city of justice is one picture of the resurrection of Christ.

In Isaiah 55 (RCL, LM), God is the host of the eschatological meal toward which the baptized journey. We are invited to a feast of free food, and the baptismal waters fill our need. The metaphor of the banquet recalls Israel's memory of being fed manna in the wilderness. God's plenteous gifts will come like rain from the sky. For the assembly, the meal is already here, offered in tonight's eucharist. The fear that Jesus is dead has been overcome by the thoughts and ways of God—for Christ is risen.

Next comes a passage from Israel's wisdom tradition (RCL, LM). Anchored in the myth of the wise king Solomon and perpetuated by generations of Jewish learning, Israelite wisdom was identified as God's gift to the chosen people. In adhering to wisdom we discover true living. In both Baruch 3 and Proverbs 8, wisdom is metaphorically described as a great woman overseeing the earth and calling the faithful into righteousness. In

Baruch, this wise woman is "the book of the precepts of God": in Proverbs, she invites everyone to her table of bread and wine, food better than fine gold. These wisdom passages were perhaps influenced by Canaanite and Egyptian goddesses who, symbolized by the tree of life, assisted with creation and bestowed wisdom. In the scriptures, the wise woman becomes a personification of God, the magnificent hostess and guide who intends justice for everyone. In later Christian tradition, she became a picture of Christ, alive in the skies, leading the faithful into truth, and inviting them to her sacred meal, a meal served both at the end of time and here at this service.

The reading in Ezekiel 36 (RCL, LM) speaks of God's relenting from punishment and saving the people by bringing them back from exile to the promised land. Like a contemporary surgeon, God provides a new heart for those who ask. Christians hear in "clean water" (v. 25) and in "a new spirit" (v. 26) references to their baptism. The promised land is both Israel's historic return from exile and, for Christians, the homeland of the church.

The RCL next appoints Ezekiel's vision in 37:1-14. Like Ezekiel, we also are surrounded by dry bones of every kind. Into this valley of death comes the divine holy breath, blowing in from the four corners of the earth, God reinvigorating creation with new life, breathing Spirit into clay. Jesus' body is no longer dry bones in a tomb, and the baptized rise to life.

The final reading from the Old Testament appointed in the RCL is Zephaniah 3:14-20. The passage is filled with images of an Easter God: God is the king, sovereign in our midst, the warrior who gives victory. God is singing. The people are called to joy, for God will restore their fortunes. Those who have disabilities and those who are outcast will be saved. Wholeness will be restored. In baptism we come home now to receive words from Paul and the narrative from the gospel.

As if all these images of God, memories of Israel, and pictures of baptism were not enough, the lectionaries assign optional communal responses to each reading, the poetry of the psalms rephrasing and amplifying the imagery of the readings. For example, following the reading from Genesis 22 is Psalm 16, which calls God our cup and our portion: we are not slain by our father, but rather we enjoy our inheritance in the promised land. The reading from the wisdom literature can be followed by Psalm 19, which praises the law as more precious than gold, sweeter than honey.

Thus, according to principle 8, the liturgies of Holy Week and Easter intend by the public reading of long biblical passages to bring the good news of Jesus' passion, death, and resurrection into the present and toward the future. Worshipers insert themselves into the narratives, receiving past salvation in the present. The designers of these lectionaries valued Christian tradition as well, searching through the centuries for the most profound ways to proclaim this good news. The readings reiterate biblical images of God, repeat Jewish memories, and apply them to Christ's resurrection and the Christian sacraments of baptism and holy communion, even relying on doublets to assist with the proclamation of the scriptures that are filled with infinitely more mercy than is easy to receive.

NOTES

1   For example, Paul F. Bradshaw and Maxwell E. Johnson, *The Origins of Feasts, Fasts, and Seasons in Early Christianity* (Collegeville, MN: Liturgical Press, 2011) and Karl Gerlach, *The Antenicene Pascha: A Rhetorical History* (Leuven, Belgium: Peeters, 1998). A summary is provided in Bonneau, *The Sunday Lectionary*, 63-77.

2   Distinctive among the many guides are James W. Farwell, *This Is the Night: Suffering, Salvation, and the Liturgies of Holy Week* (New York: T & T Clark, 2005), for setting these liturgies within the reality of human suffering; Philip H. Pfatteicher, "The Easter Vigil: Hallowing Memory," in *Liturgical Spirituality* (Valley Forge, PA: Trinity Press International, 1997), 71-104, for its emphasis on the poetic resonances in a meditative Vigil ritual; and Gail Ramshaw, *Words around the Fire: Reflections on the Scriptures of the Easter Vigil* (Chicago: Liturgy Training Publications, 1990), for prayerful commentary on the readings in the LM.

3   *Evangelical Lutheran Worship*, 269, and *Book of Common Worship*, 275.

4   See Matthew 12:40. For a discussion of catacomb and sarcophagus art, see James Stevenson, *The Catacombs: Life and Death in Early Christianity* (Nashville: Thomas Nelson, 1978), 63-84, and Robin Margaret Jensen, *Understanding Early Christian Art* (New York: Routledge, 2000), 64-93, 171-78.

5   See Anne McGowan and Paul F. Bradshaw, *The Pilgrimage of Egeria: A New Translation of the Itinerarium Egeriae with Introduction and Commentary* (Collegeville, MN: Liturgical Press, 2018).

6   For a contemporary translation of the Exultet, see "Easter Proclamation," *Evangelical Lutheran Worship, Leaders Desk Edition*, 646-47.

7   The conclusion of this volume will deal with the perceived anti-Semitism in the Bible's passion accounts.

8   See McGowan and Bradshaw, *The Pilgrimage of Egeria*.

Principle 9

ABOUT THE MYSTERY OF THE TRIUNE GOD

Go therefore and make disciples of all nations, baptizing them in the name of the Father and of the Son and of the Holy Spirit, and teaching them to obey everything that I have commanded you. And remember, I am with you always, to the end of the age.

Matthew 28:19-20

. . . .

9 The Bible serves a wide range of religious theologies and spiritualities. In the three-year lectionaries, biblical choices throughout the year affirm the mystery of the triune God.

Principle 9 in the lectionary

The three monotheistic world religions—Judaism, Christianity, and Islam—share the faith that there is one God, and only one God. At least in recent times, these religions testify that the God of each religion is the God of all three. Yet the monotheism of Christianity is unique in that the theologians of the early centuries of the church developed the doctrine of the Trinity: that the one God is a complex plural unity, revealed as Three-in-One. The Bible contains no explicit articulation of trinitarianism, but in the scriptures are the beginnings of a verbalization of trinitarian mystery. The doctrine of the triune God, finally expressed in the fourth-century theological consensus, interwove various biblical passages that spoke both separately and together of a Father, a Son, and a Spirit. Trinitarian doctrine assisted the church in affirming the divinity of Christ, and this unity of the Three in the One became the orthodox faith of the Christian tradition.[1]

Trinitarian doctrine expresses a religious mystery, for which the church does not apologize, and which the worship of the church celebrates.[2] Indeed, all monotheists maintain that divinity is beyond human comprehension and that rational human speech cannot fully articulate the being of God. Church history and current Christian practice have shown that although a three-legged stool is supposed to be the most stable, trinitarian doctrine has been difficult to maintain. According to a proposal first developed by Joachim of Fiore in the twelfth century, the age of the Father, which corresponded to the Old Testament, had been followed by the age of the Son, and finally would culminate in an apocalyptic age of the Spirit. Contemporary advocates of this suggestion see the age of the Spirit manifest in the twentieth-century rise of Pentecostalism. Perhaps religious belief would be easier were the deity solely a single being beyond the skies, or a remarkable human hero, or a universal power of life. So although all Christians acknowledge the One-in-Three, each denomination seems to have its preference, named cleverly by one author as "its Trinity affinity."[3] But for classic Christian theology, the whole Trinity is God for all times and all places.

Christians find in the scriptures the building blocks of trinitarian doctrine, and those who designed these lectionaries intended that the Sunday proclamation of the Bible manifest this threefold mystery. Although several of the passages that refer to the Three (for example, 1 Corinthians 6:11 and Luke 10:21) are not included in the three-year lectionaries, the remaining New Testament passages that contribute to the doctrine of the Trinity are in the lectionaries, spread out throughout the three years. The unfortunate practice of some preachers to announce in doleful tones that the sermon on Trinity Sunday is uniquely "about a doctrine, one that is very hard to understand," misses the point that the church's embrace by and of the triune God permeates the faith and the entire lectionary. For Christians, the Trinity was not an innovation of the New Testament, but can be glimpsed also throughout the Old Testament. The Eastern Orthodox church maintains this trinitarian interpretation in its reverence for the narrative in Genesis 18: three mysterious visitors sharing a meal with Abraham and Sarah are recognized by Christians as the one God, dining with humankind.

• •

For classic Christian theology, the whole Trinity is God for all times and all places.

• •

Classically named as Father, Son, and Spirit, the Trinity is greater than this traditional designation, and sometimes the lectionary presents the Trinity in hidden ways. For example, according to the traditional Christian interpretation of Genesis 1, the universe was created by God the Father, who spoke the word—the Word being the Son of God—and who breathed life into all things—the divine *ruah* being the Spirit: the triune God is Creator, Word, and Breath. Thus Christians see the mystery of the Trinity where others would not. The lectionaries use three techniques to affirm trinitarian faith: first, the organization of the liturgical year; second, the consistent use of three biblical selections; and third, several specifically trinitarian celebrations. We will attend to all three here.

First, historical Christianity developed a church year with three primary festivals: a Christmas that Christianized the Northern Hemisphere's winter solstice, an Easter kept near its spring equinox that Christianized the Jewish

Passover, and a Pentecost that Christianized the Jewish harvest festival. Over the centuries, some denominations and spiritualities have discarded such a liturgical year, believing that such a human invention obstructs, rather than assists, Christian faith. Some denominations have retained at least these three festivals but have dismissed most of what lies between; however, recently some such churches have added the seasons of Advent and Lent to their traditional practice, perhaps by witnessing how such a church year may indeed serve worshipers well.

The three-year lectionaries hold to the classic Western liturgical year. Throughout the course of all three years, God is manifest as the might that created the cosmos and as the fulcrum of the history of human narratives. Secondly, this God is manifest as incarnate in Jesus Christ, the commemoration of whose birth, life, passion, death, resurrection, and ascension constitutes half of the liturgical year. Thirdly, this God is experienced as the Holy Spirit, whose inspiration upholds all members of the church in its communal faith, and whose activity is explored during about half of the church year. The Trinity provides the lectionaries' skeleton each year, with the readings fleshing out the bones of trinitarian belief.

For a second trinitarian technique, each Sunday appoints three readings through which to insert the faithful into triune faith. It is relatively easy to prove almost any religious assertion one wishes, if one selects only a single biblical quote. But by submitting regularly to three readings, the church amplifies the proclamation, broadens what might be one's first reactions, and opens itself to the wideness of divine mystery. The one God comes in three. An example is the Sundays in July of year A when the gospel readings are parables of the kingdom from Matthew, which urge the faithful to be ever more faithful by following Christ in obeying the word. On several of these Sundays the second reading comes from Romans 8, Paul's powerful and resonant proclamation of the Holy Spirit, by whose might the baptized are enabled to live in God. Meanwhile, the first readings bring us the words of the prophet Isaiah, the history of the kings, the Israelite tradition of Wisdom, or God's role in the saga of Jacob. Each of these—Matthew, Paul, and the Hebrew scriptures—welcomes the others, and by holding the three together, the lectionaries, like the Trinity, convey to us a more profound religion than could each one alone.

One way that Christians have understood the Trinity is as creator, savior, and animator. So on many of the years' Sundays, the first reading presents God as the creator of the world and of the people Israel. The second reading presents God as the creator and sustainer of the church. In the gospel reading, God is the creator incarnate, the God who in the human Jesus Christ recreates humanity. Another way of looking at this is that on many of the years' Sundays, the first reading presents God as the savior of the chosen people; the second reading, God as the savior now and until the end of time; and the gospel reading, God as the savior whom we know as the Christ, Jesus of Nazareth. Or on other Sundays the first reading proclaims God as the animator of women's wombs and of the prophets' words; the second reading, God as the animator of all the baptized, even those here in this assembly; and the gospel reading, God as the animator of all things through the ministry, death, and resurrection of Christ. Thus the three readings each share in the weekly proclamation of the Trinity.

Furthermore, the lectionaries provide several sets of readings that overtly proclaim God as triune: for example, the annual Sunday of the Baptism of the Lord and, most obviously, the Sunday of the Trinity.[4] The readings on these Sundays will speak their loudest and sweetest if the Trinity has been praised as always the source, meaning, and goal of Christian worship.

Principle 9 in wider context

We live in a post-Enlightenment world, in which human reason is held up as the primary arbiter of truth. We live in an age of science and technology, in which human discoveries promise to simplify all difficulties and to solve human problems. Thus our age has an extraordinarily difficult time accepting the probability of mystery or welcoming its existence. Most of society has afforded mystery little or no space in its worldview. Occasionally a group of people band together to reject the dominant choice of science and technology, but such associations are generally dismissed as being filled with

Luddites, sadly in psychological need of what no longer exists. For hard-core atheists, belief in God is seen as an arcane attempt to escape from reality, there being no divine mystery beyond what humans are discovering.

. . . .

Christianity trusts in the mystery of Trinity.

. . . .

In contemporary speech, the word *mystery* usually denotes an entertaining puzzle. We watch a film or read a book to witness the unraveling of "a mystery," a riddle that we have not yet solved, a maze in which we have chosen to be lost. The delight comes in that we indeed will see through the mystery, for eventually such mysteries give way to our scrutiny. A list of the synonyms of the word *mystery* in current American English is instructive: enigma, problem, conundrum, mystification. Something mysterious is obscure, secret, incomprehensible, ambiguous, vague, cloudy, fuzzy, foggy, murky, opaque, convoluted, imprecise, indefinite. None of these is a good thing, none especially welcome.

One place where we do see an acknowledgement of mystery follows the increasingly common tragedy of random violence. Always the survivors ask, "Why?," for humans continuously search for meaning, and we ache to understand the threesome of the source, the meaning, and the goal of human actions. The very term *closure* suggests the conclusion of the search, the answers provided, the mystery solved. One sometimes hears talk about the mystery that follows death, but people are adept at proposing solutions to that mystery. One other mystery remains in our age of science and technology: the acknowledged mystery of each human person. Yet the phrase is seldom used in regular speech. We supply instead our Myers-Briggs score, our DNA test results.

Thus religion has an uphill climb, yet monotheisms continue to uphold the reality of mystery. Judaism reminds the faithful not to pronounce the name of God: to call out a first name is to know, and we cannot know the mystery of God. Islam offers ninety-nine names for Allah, who alone knows the hundredth name, that name of ultimate mystery. Christianity trusts in the mystery of Trinity. Each religion in its own way offers a handle for the Mystery that precedes, exemplifies, and accompanies our normal and often mundane existence.

Examples of principle 9

Baptism of the Lord (RCL, LM), Year A

On the first Sunday after Epiphany, this lectionary family celebrates the baptism of our Lord, and in all three years the narrative of Jesus' baptism proclaims the Trinity. In year A, the gospel reading for the day is Matthew 3:13-17, in which Jesus submits to John's religious ritual of cleansing in preparation for the coming of God's kingdom. Like other baptismal candidates known to the evangelist, Jesus is baptized as an adult. It is significant that the baptism takes place at the Jordan, the river that Israel had to cross as it entered the promised land. The Matthean description of the baptism is trinitarian: the heavens were opened to Jesus, thus linking the earth with the realm of God; God's voice, heard repeatedly since the creation of the earth, calls Jesus the beloved Son; and the Spirit of God descends "like a dove," alighting on Jesus. Christian tradition has seen in this narrative a picture of the Trinity: the voice, the adopted son, the dove.

As part of the interpretation of this narrative, the lectionaries appoint a first reading from Isaiah 42, the first of the four Servant Songs. For Christians, verse 1 discloses the Trinity: the church has recognized Jesus Christ in the figure of the servant, who is God's chosen, in whom God delights, and to whom God has granted the divine Spirit, so as to establish the reign of justice for all. The reading continues with praise to God, who created the earth, who gives breath and spirit to humankind, and whose covenant enlightens all things. For Christians, this enlightenment is baptism into Christ. Verse 8 names God as "Lord": this convention of biblical translation into English renders as four capital letters the tetragrammaton, YHWH, which includes the consonants in the Hebrew name of God and most probably means "I AM." Christians see God's mysterious being as this creator, this servant, this breath.

Much has been written about the response psalm, Psalm 29.[5] Scholars agree that its original form was an Ugaritic hymn in praise of the Canaanite deity Ba'al, the sky god whose voice was heard in thunder. This thundering voice issues from the highest level of the universe, the divine realm that is above the waters from which rain descends. For Christians on this Sunday, God's thunderous voice, like a hurricane breaking cedar trees and stripping forests bare, having been heard at creation, at the Red Sea, on Mount Sinai, at the Jordan, and during Jesus' baptism, speaks now at the parish baptismal font, where Christians speak their trinitarian creed. The final verse of the psalm shows the adaptation of this pagan poem for Hebrew praise of YHWH: this God, creating all things by a powerful word and a mighty spirit, promises peace.

Acts 10:34-43 is year A's second reading. The passage, cast as Peter's testimony to Cornelius, a Roman centurion, speaks of God having "anointed Jesus of Nazareth with the Holy Spirit and with power," for throughout the book of Acts, the Lukan author describes the life of the church as a continuation of the Spirit that was in Jesus Christ. Important for this third evangelist is the forgiveness of sins that is available even to Roman soldiers through the name of Jesus Christ, the incarnation of God. This Jesus preached peace and healing, descriptions Christians have given of the ministry of the Holy Spirit.

In years B and C on the Baptism of the Lord, the two branches of the lectionary appoint various readings, all of which serve the doctrine of the Trinity. In Genesis 1:1-5, God's voice and breath call life into being. In Isaiah 43:1-7, God is the Holy One of Israel, the creator, the savior, the redeemer, who will be with you in the waters. In Isaiah 55, the word of the LORD inspires the faithful to live according to God's will. In Isaiah 40, "the Lord GOD comes" with both tender care and glorious power, re-creating the land, feeding the flock, comforting the people: here also Christians see a description of the triune God. In Acts 19, Paul, preaching in Ephesus, baptizes in the name of the Lord Jesus, and "the Holy Spirit came upon them." In Acts 8, Peter and John lay hands on those who had been baptized in the name of the Lord Jesus, and they received the Holy Spirit. In 1 John 5, the baptized receive the triune God—Father, the Son of God, and the Spirit of truth. In Titus 2, the baptized are saved by "Jesus Christ our savior" and renewed by the Holy Spirit. All these various readings follow the primary path, leading from creation by God, through the incarnation of the Son, into participation in the community of the Spirit, testifying to what baptism is all about.

Trinity Sunday (RCL), Solemnity of the Most Holy Trinity (LM), Year C

Both the RCL and the LM assign to the first Sunday after Pentecost a particular focus on the Trinity. In this way, the faithful celebrate the triune God, the foundation and impetus for the second half of the liturgical year. In year C, the readings of the RCL and LM are identical. The gospel reading is John 16:12-15, a section in the fourth gospel from the longest and final of Jesus' discourses. Situated in the gospel as if spoken by Christ at the last supper, the passage is assigned by the lectionaries after Easter and Pentecost. With this placement, Jesus' words are heard as referring both to his crucifixion and to the church's life after his resurrection and ascension. Yet the good news is that the absence of Jesus from the circle of his followers will be filled with the Father's gift of Christ's Spirit of truth. The triune God is present with the faithful, for the Spirit "will guide you into all the truth." Passages such as this that describe the future of the baptized have authorized the church's historic development of doctrine. Theologians can trust that the Spirit is guiding the church, and so Christians came to interpret passages such as John 16 as proclaiming the triune God.

The first reading on Trinity year C, from Proverbs 8, like one of the readings at the Vigil of Easter, finds in the Hebrew wisdom tradition alternate language for proclaiming the Trinity. According to the metaphors in this poem, the speaker is Wisdom, a metaphorical companion of the creator before the earth was made, the master builder of all things. Christians have identified this Wisdom as the Son of God, who was with God the Father at the creation of the world. The particularly gracious final verse says that this Wisdom of God delights in the human race.

The response psalm presents a conundrum to biblical translators, especially since Psalm 8 became so historically significant to Christian theological thought. How ought the Hebrew of verse 1, naming God as both YHWH and *Adonai*, be rendered in English? What ought to be done with the original Hebrew of verses 4-6, which uses the masculine singular to refer to all humans, as androcentric languages do, so that "man" can sometimes mean "all humans"? Depending on which contemporary translation the assembly adopts, these verses refer either to all humans God has created and blessed, or to a unique "son of man," whom Christians designate as Jesus Christ. In either case, the psalm repeats praise of God's power in the creation of the world and celebrates God's majestic name.

The second reading, Romans 5:1-5, is taken from one of the earliest Christian writings. In about 57 CE, Paul wrote to the Christians in Rome that their suffering through persecution and death was bound to the suffering of Christ and thus also to his resurrection. In one of the church's first articulations of the Trinity, Paul describes the peace with God through our Lord Jesus Christ as having been poured into our hearts through the Holy Spirit. Thus God is manifest as triune, revealed through Jesus Christ and the Spirit.

Sundays of Easter (RCL, LM), Years A, B, C

The three-year lectionaries intend that the seven Sundays of Easter amplify the church's teachings about the resurrection of Jesus Christ. To do so, throughout the fifty days of Easter the first readings come from the Acts of the Apostles. In this way, Acts is heard as the chronicle of the continued divine power of the Spirit of God once seen in Christ and now alive in the church.

The RCL and the LM appoint some of the same—and some different—passages from Acts, yet in both branches of the three-year lectionary the season repeatedly testifies to the presence of the Spirit in the community of the church. In the RCL, the Spirit is explicitly cited on the third, fifth, and seventh Sundays of Easter in year A; on the fourth, fifth, sixth, and seventh Sundays in year B; and on the second, third, and fifth Sundays in year C. In the LM, we hear of the Spirit on the third, fourth, fifth, and sixth Sundays in year A; on the fourth, fifth, sixth, and seventh Sundays in year B; and on the third, fourth, sixth, and seventh Sundays in year C. The baptized community assembled to praise God stands with the risen Christ in the power of the Spirit. Easter lasts week after week, the presence of Christ experienced in the proclamation of the Trinity. For Christians, Jesus has revealed God as triune, and the three-year lectionaries celebrate that revelation.

One could certainly construct a lectionary that diminishes reference to the Trinity or indeed avoids it altogether. Such would have been the result had Thomas Jefferson assigned his edited version of the gospels to a yearlong read.[6] Biblical selections could promote a rather logical belief in a monotheistic deity whose will is manifest especially in the inspired man Jesus of Nazareth. But such is not the intention of the three-year lectionaries. Rather, it is the mystery of the Trinity that this lectionary family honors and proclaims.

NOTES

1   See J. N. D. Kelly, *Early Christian Doctrines*, 2nd ed. (New York: Harper & Row, 1958), 252-79, and Elizabeth A. Johnson, *She Who Is: The Mystery of God in Feminist Theological Discourse* (New York: Crossroad, 1992), 104-20, 191-223.

2   The classic study of mystery in the liturgy is Odo Casel, *The Mystery of Christian Worship* [1932] (Westminster, MD: Newman Press, 1962). See, for example, "The Mystery and Modern Man," 1-8.

3   Carmen Renee Berry, *The Unauthorized Guide to Choosing a Church* (Grand Rapids, MI: Brazos, 2003), 56-60 and passim.

4   For Trinity Sunday, see Ruth C. Duck and Patricia Wilson-Kastner, *Praising God: The Trinity in Christian Worship* (Louisville: Westminster John Knox, 1999), 66-80.

5   See, for example, Lowell K. Handy, ed., *Psalm 29 through Time and Tradition* (Eugene, OR: Pickwick, 2009), especially 96-97.

6   See *The Jefferson Bible*, compiled by Thomas Jefferson, 1816.

Principle 10

ABOUT A WORLDWIDE CHRISTIAN UNITY

The glory that you have given me I have given them, so that they may be one, as we are one, I in them and you in me, that they may become completely one.

John 17:22-23

. . . .

10
Christianity is a global community of faith. Use of the three-year lectionaries intensifies the participation of each individual assembly of Christians in a worldwide unity in the body of Christ.

Principle 10 in the lectionary

During the first wave of the Protestant Reformation, the Christians who became Lutherans and Anglicans retained much of the medieval Western lectionary for their Sunday worship. During the second wave of the Reformation, Ulrich Zwingli in particular rejected the historic lectionary and advocated instead that whole books of the Bible would be read at worship, chapter by chapter. It was hoped that this method would ensure that eventually the entire Bible, each page of which was believed to be inspired by the Holy Spirit for the salvation of the world, would be proclaimed. However, as is not surprising, this discipline rather quickly devolved into the practice of individual choice, as preachers skipped over those passages that were particularly obscure or had little resonance for the assembled congregation and instead pressed on toward their favorite texts. Over subsequent centuries, the proliferation of Protestant denominations, including the rise of independent churches in the twentieth century, popularized the practice that each preacher had the right—in some churches, the obligation—to select the appropriate text upon which to base the week's sermon.

For Protestants in the United States, individual choice of preaching texts became nearly sacrosanct. In this, as in many ways, Americans honored personal choice over communal consensus. The splintering of denominations had the result of exaggerating small differences in belief and biblical interpretation, and this encouraged the habit of preachers to emphasize their preferred scriptural usage. Although members of one denomination were aware that other Christian groups existed, a somewhat self-important attitude prevailed: our version of Christianity is better than yours because our use of the Bible is more faithful.

In the late twentieth century, the declining numbers of regularly worshiping church members led some denominations to strengthen their identity, which encouraged clergy to maintain the specificity of their traditions. Since a denomination, nationality, or ethnicity valued its own preferences of certain biblical patterns, then inevitably, by logical extension, so could the individual preacher. In many churches, the lone preacher's choice became all. Even in churches where the official lectionary readings were proclaimed, the sermon might begin with the line, "My text for this morning's sermon is . . . ." Sociologists describe two opposite values arising in the course of religious participation: bonding and bridging.[1] Bonding aims toward members' comfort within a known circle, bridging toward the challenge to a wider experience. To the extent that individual scriptural choice characterized preaching, churches stressed bonding: our small group was held together by its continuing biblical hermeneutic made culturally applicable by the preacher.

Meanwhile, the end of Christendom in the West led to the opposite impulse, that each small Christian group align itself with the international community of faith, gladly acknowledging itself as part of the massive worldwide association of the baptized. The ecumenical movement urged each tradition to adopt whatever it could of universal belief and practice. As in the second and third centuries, Christians could at least in some ways adopt the most universal definition of church. Since many of the distinctive congregational markers were becoming archaic, being kept alive largely as ancestral memories, a worldwide Christian identity grounded in commonalities appealed to those who were persuaded by the ecumenical movement.

The initial impetus for the three-year lectionary was not an ecumenical effort, but a Roman Catholic mandate designed for Roman Catholic churches. Yet it inspired the worldwide phenomenon of the three-year lectionaries, which are often lauded as the most influential achievement of the twentieth century's ecumenical movement. In the Lectionary for Mass, Roman Catholicism manifested a devotion to the role of scripture in the assembly that previously had been associated with Protestantism, and with the Revised Common Lectionary, many Protestant churches, intrigued by the Roman Catholic proposal, received a broader and deeper church year than had been their denominational wont. Although there are many small differences between these two major branches of the three-year lectionary tree, their essential commonality means that millions of Roman Catholic and Protestant worshiping assemblies are often hearing the same biblical readings at worship. Lectionary use no longer functions primarily as denominational bonding, but rather encourages Christian bridging.

Many assemblies using the three-year lectionary may be unaware of what a countercultural commitment this represents. The three-year lectionaries advocate for steadfast joint participation, rather than for personal preference. The American tendency to self-determination is stayed by the communal pull into a knowledge and a spirituality far beyond the self. Yes, the Spirit of God speaks to the individual, but also to the wider church, and heeding the voice of the wide community humbles any insistence that the self is the religious center.

The tenth underlying principle of the lectionary likens biblical proclamation to the very reality of life in the church. Individual Christians do not baptize themselves. We do not catechize ourselves: even when we study scripture and doctrine on our own, the biblical texts have been translated by others, and the study materials have been provided to us by centuries of believers. Religion is an endeavor communally shared, and the current desire to express that commonality in Christ finds worthy expression in a shared lectionary. Formed by ecumenical cooperation, the three-year lectionaries enact and encourage the worldwide oneness of the body of Christ.

Since at least the fourth century, the church has known two opposite methods of biblical interpretation. The pattern known as Antiochian stressed the literal meaning of the text and valued the historical situation of the presence of the Holy Spirit throughout time and place. The pattern known as Alexandrian sought a spiritual meaning of the text, valuing the ways that, through the Holy Spirit, the text enlarged and deepened the internal faith of each believer. These differences in biblical interpretation continue in our time, sometimes by denominational tradition, sometimes by personal inclination. The use of a single lectionary system does not obliterate such preferences in biblical interpretation. Rather, a shared lectionary assists both the Antiochian and the Alexandrian tendencies to recognize, even to welcome, the other as a faithful expression of God's word. As Ephraem the Syrian wrote in the fourth century:

> Many are the perspectives of God's word, just as many are the perspectives of those who study it. God has hidden in the word all kinds of treasures so that each one of us, whenever we meditate, may be enriched by it. God's utterance

is a tree of life, which offers you blessed fruit from every side. Therefore, whoever encounters one of its riches must not think that that alone which he has found is all that is in it, but rather that it is this alone that he is capable of finding from the many things in it.[2]

The three-year lectionaries encourage the churches to maintain a global communal conversation, and those who advocate such a shared lectionary see in this commitment one manifestation of the goal of Christian unity that the Johannine evangelist envisioned in the chapters known as Jesus' high priestly prayer.

It is significant that the lectionaries attend to all four gospels and to many dozens of biblical passages over a three-year period. Such a comprehensive discipline could be achieved by only a minute number of individual preachers, since given the personal preparation, inclination, and time commitments of most clergy, the texts chosen by the lone preacher or by some small group of like-minded clergy would rarely be as biblically inclusive as those appointed by the three-year lectionaries. In various places over the course of the three years—for example, in the second readings during the non-festival half of the year—this lectionary family appoints semicontinuous selections of biblical books; this dedication to consecutive biblical passages assumes weekly attention to the scriptures, a significant Christian goal. Members can be encouraged to read the designated passages of scripture alone as individuals joining with the worldwide community of the baptized if they cannot attend worship. Some of the Sunday selections appointed by the lectionaries are in themselves calls to baptismal unity, but it is also the case that the very use of the three-year lectionaries can be seen as a pledge to maintain and promote the unity of the church of Jesus Christ. Sharing these lectionaries, countless preachers and assemblies in diverse denominations practice being one in Christ.

Principle 10 in wider context

Americans tend to glorify individuality, with self-interest being a primary goal of human life.[3] "What do you want to be when you grow up?" we ask the kindergartener. We each think of ourselves as Rodin's "Thinker." On a famous episode of *Star Trek*, the alien calling out "We are Borg" is dealt with as a threat to the galaxy, but when the alien becomes an individual and learns to say "I am Hugh," the cosmos is saved and the audience cheers.[4] The Homestead Act of 1862 settled each family on its own isolated 160 acres, too far away from its neighbors to replicate the European pattern of grouping homes together in village centers surrounded by fields to which the farmer traveled each day. In a common social pattern in our day, many American young people leave home and family as a necessary step in the task of finding themselves.[5] Perhaps the desire to "be special" requires a perpetual reinvention of the individual self.[6] With well-chosen smartphone apps, the individual can now, more than ever before, imagine the powers of the self.

Henry David Thoreau is lauded for building his cabin and living alone at Walden Pond. But what is seldom mentioned is that the land Thoreau used was owned by Ralph Waldo Emerson, who purchased the acreage with the hope to protect its trees. Thoreau, however, borrowed an axe, cut down some trees, and "with the help of some of my acquaintances,"[7] set up the frame of his cabin. In American myth, Thoreau's solitude is remembered, rather than all the support he received. Significant questions are left unanswered. For example, while homeschooling nurtures the intimate unit of the family, sometimes this is done with active disregard for the wider society: How much is this for good, and how much for ill? And while individuals have the freedom to carry guns, this has opened the door to the random violence of an active shooter: When is the focus on the individual a dangerous mythic distortion of how human life actually functions in a crowded world?

Some historians and theologians credit Christianity with having invented the Western ideal of the individual. Paul preached that every single individual could receive divine grace, that each person had moral equality with all others, that each of the baptized is promised immortality. This message radically altered the social system of antiquity, in which one's birthplace in the hierarchy determined personal value.[8] While standing humbly before God, each Christian is spiritually supreme. All are invited to follow Augustine in chronicling their singular journey from, with, and toward God. For the American Enlightenment thinker Thomas Jefferson, that religious journey was in great part bounded by the self: "I am of a sect by myself," he wrote in 1819.[9] Many Americans are with Jefferson in this. For contemporary people who do join a church, their choice may be determined solely by which church best meets their personal needs. It is as if even religion "represents a frame of reference for the self."[10] It has been often suggested that the immense popularity of evangelical and free churches in our time reflects their emphasis on the individual's privileged stance before God.

Yet Paul's primary metaphor for the life of the Christian was the body of Christ. The body consists of many members: the ear needs the eye, and so on. The second and third centuries witnessed lone Christians adopting a countercultural hermit life. But for society to receive the monumental benefits effected in the Western world by this phenomenon, we need to study the later establishment of monastic communities, in which groups of equals, understanding themselves as brothers and sisters, elected their own leaders and worked together for the good of the community and the outside world.[11] It may be that humanity has had to experience the crisis of global climate change in order to take seriously the interaction between the desires of the self and the needs of the community, preferences for the present versus the requirements of the future. For a healthy—even necessary—balance between the individual and the community, humans must bond in order to bridge. As one recent philosopher has said, the appropriate question is not "Who am I?" but rather "Who are I?"[12] Even as individuals, one by one, the fact is that we contain many.

Examples of principle 10

Day of Pentecost (RCL, LM), Year A

Although the RCL provides several other optional texts for the Day of Pentecost, both the RCL and the LM include identical selections from Acts 2, 1 Corinthians 12, and John 20. To proclaim this feast, the church relies on the evangelist whom we name Luke, who wrote the only description we have of the first Christian Pentecost, which, as its title suggests, is fixed on the fiftieth day of Easter. In the Gospel according to Luke, the Spirit comes upon Mary and then Jesus, and is promised to come to all who ask (Luke 11:13), and the evangelist builds upon this theme throughout the Acts of the Apostles.

The visitation of the Holy Spirit on the entire community is set on the Jewish festival of Pentecost, which originally marked the time of the wheat harvest but over time had come to celebrate the giving of the law on Mount Sinai. In the narrative in Acts 2, the wind that throughout the Hebrew scriptures is associated with the breath of God is blowing now through the assembled community, and the fire that flamed on top of Mount Sinai is now visible on the forehead of each individual believer. The gift originally granted to a few specific persons and to one ethnic group is now granted to residents from throughout the Roman Empire—thus, to this evangelist, to the known world. What the prophet Joel saw is now made manifest to all who believe in the resurrection of Christ, for this hour of unity is likened to the apocalyptic ending of the old world. The narrative extends the faith in the resurrection from Mary Magdalene and the original disciples to "every nation under heaven," and as we hear the listing of ancient peoples and societies, we who gather around this word can realize that our own location is included. It is not surprising that in many assemblies, the proclamation of Acts 2:1-21 involves readers voicing many languages, the communities around the world brought together into one circle of Spirit power.

For the communal response to this first reading, parts of Psalm 104 are appointed, given the tradition that the Hebrew *ruah* in verse 30 is generally rendered in English as "your spirit," who renews not only the gathered assembly but also the earth itself. That is, Genesis 1 is replicated: the Holy Spirit re-creates the world. The passage from 1 Corinthians comes from Paul's discussion of religious authority and communal leadership, in which Paul's metaphor of the body of Christ is paramount. There is one body, each member having been granted some gift for the common good. As this text is proclaimed in our time, we can think of the many denominations, traditions, and spiritualities receiving the Holy Spirit and constituting the one body of Christ. When we hear Paul's list of "Jews or Greeks, slaves or free," we can think of "Orthodox, Roman Catholics, Protestants, Pentecostals, Evangelicals, and independents,"[13] all baptized into one body and drinking of one Spirit. According to the gospel reading from John 20, this Spirit came not fifty days after Easter, but on Easter Day itself, when the risen Christ appears in the assembly of the faithful, bestowing on them divine peace. In Luke, God's wind blows through the room, while in John, the risen Christ breathes on the assembled community. Thus on Pentecost the lectionary provides two ways to say the same thing.

All Saints Day (RCL), Year A; All Saints (LM), Years A, B, C

In Roman Catholicism, the festival of All Saints is a solemnity set on the traditional date of November 1. On this date in pagan times, the Celtic festival of Samhain had hoped to appease the dead so that they would stay dead and would allow the living to survive the coming winter. Since the eighth century in the West, this festival has been Christianized into the occasion to revere the saints. In medieval times, the liturgy on November 1 focused on well-known saints and martyrs, while November 2, All Souls Day, attended to all the local Christian dead. In the twentieth century, the distinction between November 1 and 2 has blurred, and many Protestant churches have welcomed November 1 into their practice as the date to thank God for all who have died in the faith. Recently, some Protestants have moved this increasingly popular commemoration to the nearest Sunday so that more people can join in the celebration.

Roman Catholics retain the practice of praying for the dead, while generally, once a funeral is over, Protestant prayer replaces supplication with thanksgiving. Yet in year A the lectionary readings for this ecumenical festival are the same in both branches of the three-year lectionary, thus holding side-by-side two different ways to remember the dead. The gospel reading is the beatitudes from Matthew 5. Writing in the 80s and summarizing themes from the preaching of Jesus, the evangelist stressed those countercultural values that the faithful are called to emulate. Other current biblical translations render the words *blessed are* as "Happy are," "You're blessed when," "How blissful are"—giving an alternate cast to this list of saints' qualities. On the festival of All Saints, the catalog of saintly characteristics calls worshipers to honor an ever-widening circle of those to whom God has given grace.

In the first reading, from Revelation 7, "a great multitude that no one could count" stands before the Lamb. The words from verse 9, "from every nation, from all tribes and peoples and languages," will remind worshipers of the reading from Acts 2 on Pentecost; such biblical passages beckon each Christian assembly to see the indescribably immense company of the saints, of which it is a tiny part. All the baptized are gathered together, their robes made white in the blood of the Lamb. One baptism has made them one.

According to the second reading, from 1 John 3, God's fatherly love has made all believers into one family of children, each one invited to become like the Son of God in faith and practice. Thus once again, as is often the case in the three-year lectionaries, the second reading pulls the current worshiping community into the biblical story: we all are the sainted children. The essay that we know as 1 John issues a strong imperative to a small group of early Christians to beware of the erroneous teachings of other groups. Yet by appointing this somewhat narrow message on All Saints, the lectionary has widened 1 John to address the whole people of God. It is hoped that, granted some ecumenical awareness of the three-year lectionaries, each worshiping assembly will realize that other churches in their neighborhood and around the world are hearing these same readings on this festival that honors all the saints of God.

Presentation of the Lord (RCL, LM), Years A, B, C

We come here to a final example of how these ten principles uphold the three-year lectionaries by considering a festival that is not a Sunday observance unless its date of February 2 falls on a Sunday. This day for worship, historically important for Roman Catholics, is now one of the six "special days" for which the RCL also appoints readings.[14] Thus the three-year lectionaries have assisted the churches in extending the understanding of Sunday to any day of the week on which the people gather around word and sacrament.

As with All Saints on November 1, this feast of the Presentation of the Lord is a Christianized Celtic observance. The celebration was originally set between the winter solstice and the spring equinox as a time to honor the goddess Brigid, who oversaw the birthing of the spring lambs and ensured the fertility of the coming agricultural year.[15] Because February 2 is forty days after Christmas, its placement invited Christians to conclude the Christmas season with a story about the infant Jesus that points to the coming seasons of Lent and Easter.

The Lukan narrative of Luke 2:22-40 has conflated two Jewish religious practices, a ritual in which the mother was cleansed of her postpartum bleeding and one in which the firstborn son was redeemed from sacrifice by means of an offering of animal substitutes. This reading calls Christians to respect the Jewish religious tradition and to recognize how it was blessed by God. The song of Simeon names Jesus as the light of both Jews and Gentiles, again a call to a worldwide unity in Christ, and the old woman Anna goes from the temple into the city to announce to everyone the coming redemption—how Lukan can you get! For as the infant Jesus is redeemed, so will all people be offered redemption, joining Anna to praise the saving God.

In Malachi 3:1-4, the first reading for Presentation of the Lord, the prophet hopes that one will come to the temple to purify the people before God more fully and finally than could any previous sacrifice. As the infant Jesus is presented in the temple, Christians smile: yes, Malachi, we see that One has indeed come to refine us into pure silver and gold. In Hebrews 2:14-18, the second reading, Christians think ahead to the passion and death of Jesus, since by his death he destroyed the power of our death. The passage from Hebrews contains the Christian religion in a nutshell: to save humans from death, God became human in Jesus so, as our brother, sharing our flesh and blood, Jesus could atone for our sins and bring us into life.

In the gospel reading, Simeon sings that now he is ready to die. One gift this festival offers to users of both the RCL and the LM is the image of the contentment that may be experienced by the believer who is contemplating death. We who are baptized can say: I am not merely an individual, naturally dreading my extinction in death. I am rather a part of the body of Christ, among the redeemed, pure silver and gold, and in that global and eternal body of Christ I can live and die in peace. Thus this festival does its part to raise us out of our individual graves and join all of us together with Simeon as he departs in peace.

NOTES

1 Putnam, *Bowling Alone*, 22.

2 Ephraem the Syrian, "Commentary on Tatian's Diatessaron," cited in Sidney H. Griffith, *Faith Adoring the Mystery: Reading the Bible with St. Ephraem the Syrian* (Milwaukee: Marquette University Press, 1997), 16-17.

3 See, for example, the extensive cultural analysis in Barry Alan Shain, *The Myth of American Individualism: The Protestant Origins of American Political Thought* (Princeton: Princeton University Press, 1994), esp. 114-50, and George Rupp, *Beyond Individualism: The Challenge of Inclusive Communities* (New York: Columbia University Press, 2015), 19-21, 76-78.

4 "I, Borg," *Star Trek: The Next Generation*, season 5, episode 23, first broadcast May 10, 1992. Excerpt available on YouTube.

5 Robert N. Bellah, et al., *Habits of the Heart: Individualism and Commitment in American Life* (Berkeley: University of California Press, 1985), 55.

6 Hal Niezviecki, *Hello, I'm Special: How Individuality Became the New Conformity* (San Francisco: City Lights, 2006).

7 Henry D. Thoreau, "Economy," *Walden*, 150th-anniversary ed. (Princeton: Princeton University Press, 2004), 45.

8 Larry Siedentop, *Inventing the Individual: The Origins of Western Liberalism* (Cambridge, MA: Belknap, Harvard University Press, 2014), 51-110.

9 Letter from Thomas Jefferson to Ezra Stiles Ely, June 25, 1819.

10 Bellah, 63.

11 Siedentop, 88-99.

12 Hélène Cixous, *The Hélène Cixous Reader*, ed. Susan Sellers (New York: Routledge, 1994), xvii.

13 For a eucharistic prayer citing all these churches, see "For All Saints," in Gail Ramshaw, *Pray, Praise, and Give Thanks: A Collection of Litanies, Laments, and Thanksgivings at Font and Table* (Minneapolis: Augsburg Fortress, 2017), 58-59.

14 See Consultation on Common Texts, *The Revised Common Lectionary*, 53-54, 108-09, 160-61.

15 See Philip H. Pfatteicher, *New Book of Festivals and Commemorations: A Proposed Common Calendar of Saints* (Minneapolis: Fortress Press, 2008), 72.

Conclusion

ACCLAIMING THE THREE-YEAR LECTIONARIES

You have been born anew, not of perishable but of imperishable seed, through the living and enduring word of God. For . . . "the word of the Lord endures forever." That word is the good news that was announced to you.

1 Peter 1:23-25

Many Christians around the world join me in advocating for the three-year lectionaries. Some of the advocates are clergy who find in the biblical selections an ongoing inspiration for their weekly task of preaching. Others are laypersons like me, who never preach, and yet who are grateful for the continual growth in grace offered through these lectionaries' readings, whether encountered during assembly worship, in parish lectionary studies, or in private home devotions, and they find it a joy to experience a unity of the body of Christ when, worshiping in a distant place or another denomination, they discover there the same readings they would experience at home.

The grace offered through these lectionaries is plentiful. By means of this lectionary family, we receive the witness to Jesus Christ from all four gospels. When we weary of Matthew urging us to obedience, there comes Mark, who acknowledges the weakness of all disciples; and as we admit our frailty, we welcome Luke, who offers us forgiveness, even from the cross; and throughout each year, John invites us into the heights and depths of divine mystery. Along with the gospels are many of the biblical books, heard in such a way as to honor the triune God through Christ. The psalms feed us with the manna of metaphor. We join with the baptized of many denominations to keep the whole Christian year, Sunday after Sunday, from one Advent to the next. If all church members have a copy of the lectionary listing at home, they can prepare for each Sunday's reading in the days before, and we trust that the hymns, all the music, the printed or projected art, the adornments of space itself, Sunday's adult Bible study, and the children's curriculum will complement the readings, just as our very lives are called to do.

However, now it is time to address at least some of the criticisms that are aimed at this lectionary family. Some criticisms that are voiced are wholly personal: for example, sadness that one's favorite biblical stories or passages are omitted. Yet even the critics know that lectionaries cannot include the entire scriptures. Some criticisms may reflect the considerable distance between what the three-year lectionaries present and what the preachers learned at seminary concerning the task of weekly proclamation—for example, the understanding that a sermon ought to expound on only a single biblical passage. It may be that the intensive biblical study that the lectionaries encourage will take more time than some clergy wish to dedicate to this aspect of their ministry, and a preliminary acquaintance with the lectionary will indicate only the work required, not the benefits accrued.

Some hermeneutical issues that are raised concerning the three-year lectionaries would touch upon any lectionary.[1] Who determines the canon within the canon that a lectionary promotes? Ought individual biblical passages be linked with others and across the two testaments? Is John handled correctly? Are the readings too short? Are the readings too lengthy? Is the core content of Jesus' proclamation represented accurately? Does Judaism figure appropriately? Is there sufficient attention given to women, to people with disabilities, to those who are oppressed, to political realities, to the wisdom tradition, to creation, to care for the earth, to divine punishment? Are the choices too tame? Does the use of a denominational lectionary grant the church leadership too much authority?

To summarily list critical questions such as these is not to diminish their significance for the church's faithful proclamation of the word of God. The ordained clergy rightly bear the responsibility to preach the "word of God" with earnest clarity, and as the "word of life" the Bible must be heard addressing these and many other issues. Yet it is unlikely that a single lectionary, even one lasting three years, could answer all such inquiries to the satisfaction of everyone since focus on some of these issues precludes focus on others. A lectionary is a zero-sum game—one new reading in, one existing reading out—that intends to address Christians of all ages, languages, nations, cultures, historic traditions, and spiritual pieties around the world. To construct a worldwide lectionary is a worthy goal, but one exceedingly difficult to achieve to everyone's satisfaction.

However, a lectionary is only a foundation upon which the baptized community builds. It is hoped that Christians who mourn the absence of some passages or interpretive techniques will expand their biblical studies beyond Sunday morning, relying on other venues, such as Bible study classes, midweek services, day-long retreats, summer camps, or home devotions, to give those preferences currency. Given the amount of investment made by some denominational publishing houses in three-year lectionary resources, it is not likely that substantial changes to these lectionaries will come about any time soon.

There is, however, one grave criticism of these lectionaries that demands close attention here, and that is the matter of the inclusion of readings that are perceived by many hearers in our time as anti-Semitic. Throughout the scriptures are proper nouns that had a different referent in the past than in the present. Undoubtedly, all lectionaries would include some passages in which "Jerusalem" is extravagantly lauded or "Israel" is harshly condemned, and it may be that hearers could confuse the biblical Jerusalem with the current Jerusalem, Israel in the past with Israel in the present. It may be that in our time the noun "Pharisee" has become merely a synonym for "hypocrite" and so is no longer heard as it would have been in the year 100, when the Pharisees had become the dominant Jews of the period. But how does a contemporary worshiping assembly interpret those Old Testament readings, for example, that scold "Israel" for being stiff-necked? In the face of such texts, preaching to the baptized needs to make clear that it is the present assembly that is stiff-necked: both biblical condemnations and commendations address the present assembly. For contemporary Christians to receive the good news by means of an ancient text, biblical proclamation always requires insightful preaching and pertinent education, perhaps assisted by helpful definitions provided in the worship folder.

Most often, this concern is focused on the noun *Jew*. In our time, this word has many referents: an adherent of the religion of Judaism; a member of a historic ethnicity; a participant, by birth or choice, in a cultural community; a subject of an ancient religious and ethnic nation-state; even a citizen of the state of Israel. Most English biblical translations use this multivalent noun— "the Jews"—to render the New Testament's Greek noun *Ioudaioi*, literally "Judeans," and thus the gospels' accounts of Jesus' passion and death might be heard as blaming "the Jews" for the death of Christ.

Biblical scholars have struggled to agree on the actual legal charges that led to Jesus' conviction.[2] Whatever were the facts of the trial, Christian theology has at its best taught that it was our sins that led to Jesus' death. Yet worshipers, hearing in Matthew 27:25 the mob assuming blame for his conviction, in Luke 23 the role played by the Judean Herod, and the repeated references to "the Jews" in John 18–19, may perpetuate the historic anti-Semitism that all lectionaries ought to decry. Some biblical translations attempt to clarify the participants in these narratives by word choices such as "the crowd," "the temple authorities," or "the Jewish leaders," and these translations may render the passages less prone to misunderstanding.[3]

· ·

Each foundational principle has to some degree addressed a significant criticism of the three-year lectionaries.

· ·

Because in the three-year lectionaries two passion accounts are proclaimed each year, a synoptic account on Passion Sunday and the Johannine account on Good Friday, worshipers will hear two somewhat different versions of Christ's arrest, trial, execution, death, and burial. It may be that exposure to the doublet increases the likelihood that local assemblies will engage in study of these passages, to attend to the issues of translation and the dangers of historic anti-Semitism. Recently it has sometimes been suggested that, given the length of the passion accounts, preaching can be omitted on Passion Sunday and Good Friday. However, such advice vastly underestimates the complexity of the many historical, theological, and spiritual issues encountered in these texts. The passion accounts—as much as, if not more than, all biblical readings—cry out for responsible treatment by the preacher. Thus while the issue of perceived anti-Semitism remains of concern with the three-year lectionaries, any and all biblical readings of Jesus' arrest, trial, and crucifixion rely on informed catechesis for appropriate reception by believers.

In this volume, each foundational principle has to some degree addressed a significant criticism of the three-year lectionaries. For example, one criticism of this lectionary family is that, given that the Bible contains far more material than only testimony to Jesus, the lectionary is too Christological. This criticism is addressed in chapter 1 by its discussion of the principle that this lectionary is designed for use at Christian assemblies on the day of Christ's resurrection, thus rendering the choices unabashedly Christological. Principle 1 is intended to convince readers of the merits of a Christological focus.

A second criticism is that, despite the considerable doubt cast by contemporary theologians on the historicity of the scriptures, the three-year lectionaries do not contain enough Bible: in chapter 2, the second principle describes the choices employed when proclaiming what of biblical memory is most important for Christian faith and life. A third criticism, that the Old Testament ought not be viewed through a Christian lens, is dealt with in chapter 3.[4] According to principle 3, at assembly worship the baptized community gathers to become strengthened in their faith, and so their reading of the Hebrew scriptures ought logically to relate to that goal. Recently there has been concern that not enough psalm laments are appointed for regular Christian prayer; the specific Sunday use of the psalter is addressed in chapter 4. Of course, principle 4 does not mean to suggest that Sunday usage is the sole way Christians will pray the psalms: other contexts and other purposes will employ the psalms in other ways.[5]

· ·

By the expression of these ten principles, the three-year lectionaries have given the churches the most comprehensive lectionary that has thus far been advanced.

· ·

The criticism that the churches' contemporary issues, which change decade by decade, are not sufficiently covered in the lectionaries' biblical selections is discussed in chapter 5, and the many available preaching guides to the lectionaries provide ample models for recognizing how current issues are found in ancient texts. Some critics maintain that the classic four weeks of Advent and the twelve days of Christmas are no longer liturgically useful patterns in our time, and this issue is addressed in principle 6. Some critics urge that, in accord with the dominant Western historic tradition, Lent should continue to focus solely on personal sinfulness, rather than the lectionaries' attention to the baptismal journey: principle 7 has sought to address this issue. We have dealt here and in principle 8 with one of the most problematic issues: how the Gospel according to John is best understood without anti-Semitic overtones. That the doctrine of the Trinity ought not be superimposed upon the Bible is an opinion that is dealt with in principle 9, which claims that for Christians, a trinitarian faith rightly derives from and is nurtured by the scriptures. That free choice of biblical readings is better than ecumenical concurrence is discussed both in principle 10 and in the sections "in wider context," as the honor to the community is contrasted with the preference for the self.

It may be the case that the chapter discussions of the implications of these ten principles are not as convincing as the author hopes. But the author has made the effort to maintain that, given its foundational principles, the three-year lectionary is its own defense, its choices reflecting its undeniably Christian principles.

One way to define religion is as (1) a communal worldview (2) about ultimate reality (3) with requisite rituals (4) and ensuing ethics.[6] This volume has addressed the third feature especially, that its religious rituals cultivate the worldview that bears a particular understanding of ultimate meaning and religious ethics. A Christian lectionary means to address these issues as profoundly and creatively as it can, its choices of readings from its sacred scriptures seen to nurture a worldwide community in the faith of the triune God and in loving service to others. No lectionary will be perfect, able to please the countless preachers, musicians, catechists, and lay worshipers of numerous denominations and pieties around the Christian world. Yet by the expression of these ten principles, the three-year lectionaries have given the churches the most comprehensive lectionary that has thus far been advanced.

In a masterful prayer composed by Thomas Cranmer in the mid-sixteenth century, we praise God for the holy scriptures, and we pray that we may "hear them, read, mark, learn, and inwardly digest them."[7] Cranmer, a genius at crafting the prose of Christian liturgy, lived and died through the sorrowful Catholic-Protestant conflicts of earlier centuries. But thanks to the work of the Holy Spirit, these churches have now been given the ecumenical banquet of the three-year lectionaries as the primary way to consume and digest what is now often called "the richer fare" of the scriptures.[8] No longer killing one another, we Christians are coming to be united in the word. Together the churches can plant the seed of the word and watch it grow into that tree of life described by the seer in Revelation 22, with its twelve different kinds of fruit and leaves that heal the nations.

Foundational principles of the three-year lectionaries

1 The fundamental Christian ritual is held on Sunday, because Sunday is the day of Christ's resurrection. In the three-year lectionaries, the resurrection undergirds every Sunday, as well as the fifty days of the Easter season.

2 Many Christians agree that a passage from a gospel is the primary reading on each Sunday and festival. Because the four gospels narrate the story of Jesus Christ in different ways, the three-year lectionaries appoint readings from all four.

3 Given the fact of biblical intertextuality, the Hebrew scriptures provide necessary context for understanding the Christian scriptures. In the three-year lectionaries, the gospel readings are linked with selections from the Old Testament.

4 Since the beginnings of the church, the psalms and other biblical canticles have served Christians as poetic praise and prayer. In the three-year lectionaries, the assembly participates in the proclamation of scripture by singing a psalm or canticle as a metaphorical response to the first reading or to the day as a whole.

5 A living religion speaks out of the past into the present and the future. In the three-year lectionaries, a selection from the New Testament writings typifies the church's focus on the meaning of Christ for contemporary Christian living.

6 Christians observe the season of Advent as preparation for the coming of God in Christ. In the three-year lectionaries, the Advent readings express the many human longings that manifest our ultimate longing for God.

7 Many Christians prepare for the annual observances of Holy Week and Easter by keeping the season of Lent. In the three-year lectionaries, Lent focuses on baptismal identity and the consequent amendment of life.

8 Holy Week and Easter have been observed in many ways since their origin in the second century as the Christianized Passover. In the three-year lectionaries, Holy Week and the Easter paschal celebrations bring both the biblical and the liturgical past into the present.

9 The Bible serves a wide range of religious theologies and spiritualities. In the three-year lectionaries, biblical choices throughout the year affirm the mystery of the triune God.

10 Christianity is a global community of faith. Use of the three-year lectionaries intensifies the participation of each individual assembly of Christians in a worldwide unity in the body of Christ.

NOTES

1   Raymer, "The Synoptic Lectionaries: Criticism," in *The Bible in Worship*, 178-203.

2   See, for example, Raymond E. Brown, *The Death of the Messiah* (New York: Doubleday, 1994), vol. 1, 753-59, 778-86, 859-61.

3   One such emendation is provided in *Sundays and Seasons: Guide to Worship Planning, Year A 2020* (Minneapolis: Augsburg Fortress, 2019), 142-45.

4   This is one way to view the concerns of Amy-Jill Levine, "Listening to Jesus as a Jew," *The Christian Century*, 136, no. 7 (March 27, 2019): 27-29.

5   See, for example, Gail Ramshaw, "The Brutal Brilliance of the Psalms," *Call to Worship* 52, no. 3 (2019): 16-21.

6   For this definition, see Gail Ramshaw, *Under the Tree of Life: The Religion of a Feminist Christian* (New York: Continuum, 1998), v-vi.

7   *The Collects of Thomas Cranmer*, C. Frederick Barbee and Paul F. M. Zahl, eds. (Grand Rapids, MI: William B. Eerdmans, 1999), 4.

8   See Second Vatican Council, *The Constitution on the Sacred Liturgy*, (Collegeville, MN: Liturgical Press, 1963), II, 51.

ACKNOWLEDGMENTS

My interest in lectionary began back in elementary school, when I discovered in *The Lutheran Hymnal* that my denomination prescribed more Bible and a fuller church year than did my pastor. At Valparaiso University, I encountered *The Year of Grace* by Pius Parsch, and for my student aide job I prepared the Sunday's intercessions for campus worship. And although I am a Lutheran laywoman who never preaches in the assembly, for over half a century I have been supported in my devotion to the lectionary by many persons: Daniel Brockopp † of the Valparaiso University chapel; Alexander Schmemann † of St. Vladimir's Orthodox Theological Seminary; Robert V. Schnabel † of Concordia College, Bronxville; Raymond E. Brown, SS, † of Union Theological Seminary; Eugene Brand at the Lutheran Church in America; Bernard Benziger † of Pueblo Publishing Company; Gabe Huck while at Liturgy Training Publications; the members of the Consultation on Common Texts; a drafting committee for *Evangelical Lutheran Worship*; the participants of the Liturgical Language seminar of the North American Academy of Liturgy; journal editors Kevin Seasoltz, OSB †, Bernadette Gasslein, and Melinda Quivik; David Gambrell and Kimberly Bracken Long of the Presbyterian Church U.S.A.; over the years, Samuel Torvend, Frank Stoldt, Robert Buckley Farlee, Suzanne Burke, and Jennifer Baker-Trinity, editors at Augsburg Fortress; and Kevin Strickland, then executive for worship of the Evangelical Lutheran Church in America, and now bishop of the Southeastern Synod. To all of these, and to Gordon Lathrop for continuous conversation about the lectionary readings, I express my gratitude beyond measure.

I am indebted to Augsburg Fortress editor Laurie J. Hanson, especially for the pull quotes; to Tory Herman, the page designer and typesetter; and to Laurie Ingram, the cover designer.

Now and again, Martin Seltz, vice president and publisher of congregational resources at 1517 Media, would say to me, "And Gail, when are you going to write that book about the lectionary?" Thank you, Martin: this one's for you.

BIBLIOGRAPHY

Primary sources

Consultation on Common Texts. *The Revised Common Lectionary*. 20th-anniversary annotated ed. Minneapolis: Fortress Press, 2012.

Lectionary for Mass. Study ed. Vol. 1: *Sundays, Solemnities, Feasts of the Lord and the Saints*. Collegeville, MN: Liturgical Press, 2000.

Further resources and weekly lectionary guides

Allen, Horace T., Jr., and Joseph P. Russell. *On Common Ground: The Story of the Revised Common Lectionary*. Norwich, UK: Canterbury Press, 1998.

Bartlett, David, and Barbara Brown Taylor. *Feasting on the Word: Preaching the Revised Common Lectionary*. 12 vols. Louisville: Westminster John Knox Press, 2011.

Bonneau, Normand. *The Sunday Lectionary: Ritual Word, Paschal Shape*. Collegeville, MN: Liturgical Press, 1998.

Bower, Peter C., ed. *Handbook for the Revised Common Lectionary*. Louisville: Westminster John Knox Press, 1996.

Evangelical Lutheran Church in America (ELCA). *Evangelical Lutheran Worship*. Minneapolis: Augsburg Fortress, 2006.

———. *Evangelical Lutheran Worship, Leaders Desk Edition*. Minneapolis: Augsburg Fortress, 2006.

Fuller, Reginald H. *Preaching the Lectionary: The Word of God for the Church Today*. 3rd ed. Collegeville, MN: Liturgical Press, 2006.

Green, Joel B., Thomas G. Long, Luke A. Powery, and Cynthia L. Rigby, eds. *Connections: A Lectionary Commentary for Preaching and Worship*. Louisville: Westminster John Knox Press, 2018—.

Lawrence, Kenneth T., ed. *Imaging the Word: An Arts and Lectionary Resource*. Cleveland: United Church Press, 1994–97.

Nocent, Adrien. *The Liturgical Year*. 3 vols. Translated by Matthew J. O'Connell. Introduced, emended, and annotated by Paul Turner. Collegeville, MN: Liturgical Press, 2013, 2014.

Nowell, Irene. *Sing a New Song: The Psalms in the Sunday Lectionary*. Collegeville, MN: Liturgical Press, 1993.

O'Day, Gail R., and Charles Hackett. *Preaching the Revised Common Lectionary: A Guide*. Nashville: Abingdon Press, 2007.

O'Loughlin, Thomas. *Making the Most of the Lectionary: A User's Guide*. London: SPCK, 2012.

Raymer, Victoria. *The Bible in Worship: Proclamation, Encounters and Response*. London: SCM Press, 2018.

Stancliffe, David. *The Gospels in Art, Music, and Literature: The Story of Salvation in Three Media*. 3 vols. London: SPCK, 2013, 2014, 2015.

The Sunday Website at Saint Louis University. Catholic Studies Program. http://liturgy.slu.edu.

Sundays and Seasons: Guide to Worship Planning. Minneapolis: Augsburg Fortress. An annual guide. Also: sundaysandseasons.com. A subscription website for worship planners.

"Sunday's Coming." *The Christian Century*. https://www.christiancentury.org/blog/sundays-coming. Weekly lectionary email and blog post.

The United Methodist Church. *The United Methodist Hymnal: Book of United Methodist Worship*. Nashville: United Methodist Publishing House, 1989.

Van Harn, Roger E., and Brent A. Strawn, eds. *Psalms for Preaching and Worship: A Lectionary Commentary*. Grand Rapids, MI: William B. Eerdmans, 2009.

West, Fritz. *Scripture and Memory: The Ecumenical Hermeneutic of the Three-Year Lectionaries*. Collegeville, MN: Liturgical Press, 1997.

Woodard, Jenee. *The Text This Week*. https://www.textweek.com.

Additional works cited

Alexander, J. Neil. *Waiting for the Coming: The Liturgical Meaning of Advent, Christmas, Epiphany*. Washington, DC: Pastoral Press, 1993.

Appiah, Kwame Anthony. *The Lies That Bind: Rethinking Identity*. New York: Liveright Publishing Corporation, 2018.

Augustine. *Confessions*, Translated by Henry Chadwick. Oxford, UK: Oxford University Press, 1991.

Bandy, Thomas G. *Introducing the Uncommon Lectionary: Opening the Bible to Seekers and Disciples*. Nashville: Abingdon, 2006.

Barrois, Georges. *Scripture Readings in Orthodox Worship*. Crestwood, NY: St. Vladimir's Seminary Press, 1977.

Bellah, Robert N., Richard Madsen, William M. Sullivan, Ann Swidler, and Steven M. Tipton. *Habits of the Heart: Individualism and Commitment in American Life*. Berkeley: University of California Press, 1985.

Berry, Carmen Renee. *The Unauthorized Guide to Choosing a Church*. Grand Rapids, MI: Brazos Press, 2003.

Boeve, Lieven. "Symbols of Who We Are Called to Become: Sacraments in a Post-Secular and Post-Christian Society." *Studia Liturgica* 48 (2018): 154-55.

Boulding, Maria. *The Coming of God*. 3rd ed. Conception, MO: Printery House, 2000.

Bradshaw, Paul F., and Maxwell E. Johnson. *The Origins of Feasts, Fasts, and Seasons in Early Christianity*. Collegeville, MN: Liturgical Press, 2011.

Brown, Raymond E. *The Birth of the Messiah: A Commentary on the Infancy Narratives in Matthew and Luke*. Garden City, NY: Doubleday, 1977.

———. *Christ in the Gospels of the Liturgical Year*. Expanded edition. Collegeville, MN: Liturgical Press, 2008.

———. *The Death of the Messiah*. New York: Doubleday, 1994.

———. *The Gospel according to John*. Vol. 1. Garden City, NY: Doubleday, 1966.

Brown, William P. *Seeing the Psalms: A Theology of Metaphor*. Louisville: Westminster John Knox Press, 2002.

Brueggemann, Walter. *Names for the Messiah: An Advent Study*. Louisville: Westminster John Knox Press, 2016.

Casel, Odo. *The Mystery of Christian Worship* [1932]. Westminster, MD: The Newman Press, 1962.

Cixous, Hélène. *The Hélène Cixous Reader*. Edited by Susan Sellers. New York: Routledge, 1994.

Collins, Raymond F. *Preaching the Epistles*. New York: Paulist Press, 1996.

Connell, Martin. *Guide to the Revised Lectionary*. Chicago: Liturgy Training Publications, 1998.

Cranmer, Thomas. *The Collects of Thomas Cranmer*. Edited by C. Frederick Barbee and Paul F. M. Zahl. Grand Rapids, MI: William B. Eerdmans, 1999.

Daniélou, Jean. *The Bible and the Liturgy*. Notre Dame: University of Notre Dame Press, 1956.

Day, Dorothy. *Reflections during Advent: On Prayer, Poverty, Chastity, and Obedience*. Lawrence Cunningham. Notre Dame, IN: Ave Maria Press, 1966.

Duck, Ruth C., and Patricia Wilson-Kastner. *Praising God: The Trinity in Christian Worship*. Louisville: Westminster John Knox, 1999.

Dueholm, Benjamin J. *Sacred Signposts: Words, Water, and Other Acts of Resistance*. Grand Rapids, MI: William B. Eerdmans, 2018.

The Episcopal Church. *The Book of Common Prayer*. New York: Seabury Press, 1977.

Farwell, James W. *This Is the Night: Suffering, Salvation, and the Liturgies of Holy Week*. New York: T & T Clark, 2005.

Gerlach, Karl. *The Antenicene Pascha: A Rhetorical History*. Leuven, Belgium: Peeters, 1998.

Gooder, Paula. *The Meaning Is in the Waiting: The Spirit of Advent*. Brewster, MA: Paraclete Pres, 2009.

Goppelt, Leonard. *Typos: The Typological Interpretation of the Old Testament in the New*. Translated by Donald H. Madvig. Grand Rapids, MI: William B. Eerdmans, 1982.

Griffith, Sidney H. *Faith Adoring the Mystery: Reading the Bible with St. Ephraem the Syrian*. Milwaukee: Marquette University Press, 1997.

Habel, Norman. *The Key to the Purple Puzzle Tree*. St. Louis: Concordia Publishing House, 1973.

Handy, Lowell K., ed. *Psalm 29 through Time and Tradition*. Eugene, OR: Pickwick Publications, 2009.

Harland, Philip A. *Associations, Synagogues, and Congregations: Claiming a Place in Ancient Mediterranean Society*. Minneapolis: Fortress Press, 2003.

Harline, Craig. *Sunday: A History of the First Day from Babylonia to the Super Bowl*. New York: Doubleday, 2007.

Hayden, Brian. *Shamans, Sorcerers, and Saints: A Prehistory of Religion*. Washington: Smithsonian Books, 2003.

Holland, Melford "Bud." *Advent Presence: Kissed by the Past, Beckoned by the Future*. New York: Morehouse, 2015.

Holmes, Stephen Mark, ed. *The Fathers on the Sunday Gospels*. Collegeville, MN: Liturgical Press, 2012.

Hunt, Patricia J. *The All Color Book of Bible Stories*. London, UK: Hennerwood Publications, 1978.

Irenaeus. "Against Heresies," *Early Christian Fathers*. Translated and edited by Cyril C. Richardson. New York: Macmillan, 1970.

Jensen, Robin Margaret. *Understanding Early Christian Art*. New York: Routledge, 2000.

Johnson, Elizabeth A. *She Who Is: The Mystery of God in Feminist Theological Discourse*. New York: Crossroad Publishing Company, 1992.

Kähler, Martin. *The So-Called Historical Jesus and the Historic, Biblical Christ* [1896]. Translated by Carl E. Braaten. Philadelphia: Fortress Press, 1964.

Kelly, J. N. D. *Early Christian Doctrines*. 2nd ed. New York: Harper & Row, 1958.

Kraybill, Donald B., Steven M. Nolt, and David L. Weaver-Zercher. *The Amish Way: Patient Faith in a Perilous World*. San Francisco: Jossey-Bass, 2010.

Lakoff, George, and Mark Johnson. *Metaphors We Live By*. Chicago: University of Chicago Press, 2003.

Lathrop, Gordon W. *Central Things: Worship in Word and Sacrament*. Minneapolis: Augsburg Fortress, 2005.

―――. *The Four Gospels on Sunday: The New Testament and the Reform of Christian Worship*. Minneapolis: Fortress Press, 2012.

―――. *Proclamation 4, Advent/Christmas*, series B. Minneapolis: Fortress Press, 1990.

―――. *Saving Images: The Presence of the Bible in Christian Liturgy*. Minneapolis: Fortress Press, 2017.

Levine, Amy-Jill. "Listening to Jesus as a Jew." *The Christian Century* 136, no. 7 (March 27, 2019): 27-29.

Lutheran-Roman Catholic Commission on Unity. *From Conflict to Communion: Lutheran-Catholic Common Commemoration of the Reformation in 2017*. Leipzig: Evangelische Verlagsanstalt, 2013.

Martin, Raymond, and John Barresi. *The Rise and Fall of Soul and Self*. New York: Columbia University Press, 2006.

McDonald, Lee Martin. *Formation of the Bible: The Story of the Church's Canon*. Peabody, MA: Hendrickson Publishers, 2012.

McGowan, Andrew B. *Ancient Christian Worship: Early Church Practices in Social, Historical, and Theological Perspective*. Grand Rapids, MI: Baker Academic, 2014.

McGowan, Anne, and Paul F. Bradshaw. *The Pilgrimage of Egeria: A New Translation of the Itinerarium Egeriae with Introduction and Commentary*. Collegeville, MN: Liturgical Press, 2018.

Melito. *Melito of Sardis: On Pascha and Fragments*. Edited by Stuart George Hall. Oxford: Clarendon, 1979.

Mittelberger, Gottlieb. "Journey to Pennsylvania." In *Pennsylvania Dutch: Folk Spirituality*, edited by Richard W. Wentz, 72-78. New York: Paulist Press, 1993.

Nicolet-Anderson, Valérie. *Constructing the Self: Thinking with Paul and Michel Foucault*. Tübingen, Germany: Mohr Siebeck, 2012.

Niezviecki, Hal. *Hello, I'm Special: How Individuality Became the New Conformity*. San Francisco: City Lights, 2006.

Nilsson, Nils-Henrik. "The Principles behind the New Sunday Lectionary for the Church of Sweden." *Studia Liturgica* 34 (Sept. 2004): 240-50.

O'Collins, Gerald. *All Things New: The Promise of Advent, Christmas and the New Year*. New York: Paulist Press, 1998.

Parsch, Pius. *The Church's Year of Grace*. Translated by William G. Heidt. Vol. 1, *Advent to Candlemas*. Collegeville, MN: Liturgical Press, 1959.

Petersen, William H. *What Are We Waiting For? Re-Imaging Advent for Time to Come*. New York: Church Publishing House, 2017.

Pfatteicher, Philip H. "The Easter Vigil: Hallowing Memory." In *Liturgical Spirituality*, 71-104. Valley Forge, PA: Trinity Press International, 1997.

———. *New Book of Festivals and Commemorations: A Proposed Common Calendar of Saints*. Minneapolis: Fortress Press, 2008.

Polkinghorne, John. *Living with Hope: A Scientist Looks at Advent, Christmas, and Epiphany*. Louisville: Westminster John Knox Press, 2003.

Potts, Richard, and Christopher Sloan. *What Does It Mean to Be Human?* Washington, DC: National Geographic, 2010.

Presbyterian Church (U.S.A.). *The Book of Common Worship*. Louisville: Westminster John Knox Press, 2018.

———. *Glory to God*. Louisville: Westminster John Knox Press, 2013.

Putnam, Robert D. *Bowling Alone: The Collapse and Revival of American Community*. New York: Simon & Schuster, 2000.

Ramshaw, Gail. "The Brutal Brilliance of the Psalms." *Call to Worship* 52, no. 3 (2019): 16-21.

———. "The First Testament in Christian Lectionaries." *Worship* 64 (1990): 494-510.

———. *Pray, Praise, and Give Thanks: A Collection of Litanies, Laments, and Thanksgivings at Font and Table*. Minneapolis: Augsburg Fortress, 2017.

———. *A Three-Year Banquet: The Lectionary for the Assembly*. Minneapolis: Augsburg Fortress, 2004.

———. *Under the Tree of Life: The Religion of a Feminist Christian*. New York: Continuum, 1998.

———. *Words around the Fire: Reflections on the Scriptures of the Easter Vigil*. Chicago: Liturgy Training Publications, 1990.

Rappaport, Roy A. *Ritual and Religion in the Making of Humanity*. Cambridge, UK: Cambridge University Press, 1999.

Ricoeur, Paul. *The Rule of Metaphor: Multi-disciplinary Studies of the Creation of Meaning in Language*. Translated by Robert Czerny. Toronto: University of Toronto Press, 1977.

Rordorf, Willy. *Sunday: The History of the Day of Rest and Worship in the Earliest Centuries of the Christian Church*. Philadelphia: Westminster Press, 1968.

Rosner, Brian S. *Known by God: A Biblical Theology of Personal Identity*. Grand Rapids, MI: Zondervan, 2017.

Rupp, George. *Beyond Individualism: The Challenge of Inclusive Communities*. New York: Columbia University Press, 2015.

Second Vatican Council. *The Constitution on the Sacred Liturgy*. Collegeville, MN: Liturgical Press, 1963.

Shain, Barry Alan. *The Myth of American Individualism: The Protestant Origins of American Political Thought*. Princeton: Princeton University Press, 1994.

Siedentop, Larry. *Inventing the Individual: The Origins of Western Liberalism*. Cambridge, MA: Belknap, Harvard University Press, 2014.

Skudlarek, William. *The Word in Worship: Preaching in a Liturgical Context*. Nashville: Abingdon, 1981.

Spier, Peter. *Noah's Ark*. New York: Doubleday & Company, 1977.

Stevens, Wallace. *Opus Posthumous*. Edited by Samuel French Morse. New York: Knopf, 1966.

Stevenson, James. *The Catacombs: Life and Death in Early Christianity*. Nashville: Thomas Nelson, 1978.

Thoreau, Henry D. "Economy." *Walden*. 150th-anniversary ed. Princeton: Princeton University Press, 2004.

Uro, Risto. *Ritual and Christian Beginnings: A Socio-Cognitive Analysis*. Oxford, UK: Oxford University Press, 2016.

Vorster, Willem S. "Intertextuality and Redaktionsgeschichte." In *Intertextuality in Biblical Writings*, edited by Sipke Draisma, 15-26. Kampen: Uitgeversmaatschappij J.H. Kok, 1989.

Weren, Wilhelmus Johannes Cornelis. *Studies in Matthew's Gospel: Literary Design, Intertextuality, and Social Setting*. Leiden: Brill, 2014.

INDEX

Primary examples from the three-year lectionaries